Contents

LARF MATTERS	1
Adam And Eve – the true story	6
Adult Thoughts	7
Advice Columns – why men shouldn't write them	8
Age Concerns	9
Age and Restaurants	11
Alphabet – Cockney	12
Alzheimers Test	13
Amish Anti-Ageing	14
Aussie And The Emu	15
Aviation Problems	17
Aviation Rules	19
Beard Facts	21
Beneficiary Letters	22
Billy Connoly Questions	23
Black Testicles	24
Blondes	25
Bureaucratic Wisdom	27
California	28
Childrens' Answers	30
Children's Fairy Story	31
Child Wisdom	32
Child Wisdom … On Love	33
Child Wisdom … On Religion	35
Christmas Party Invitation	39
Classical Gaffes	42
Computer Company Memo	43
Computer Dictionary For Kiwis (New Zealanders)	44
Consumer Labels	45

Corporate Capabilities	47
Cowboy Wisdom	48
Do You Know?	50
Discovery Of Radio	52
Dog's Rules	53
Donkey Types	56
Dumb And Dumber	57
Elder Wisdom I	59
Elder Wisdom II	61
Elder Q & A Forum	62
Email Disclaimer	64
English Language Improvements	66
English Language Backwards	67
Fairy Tale For Men	68
Famous Names In History	69
Finishing Things For Calm	70
First Date	71
Friendship Poem	73
George W. Bush Wisdom	74
God's Children	76
God's Grass	77
Hell Freezing Over	79
Health Tips	81
Interesting And Useless Facts	83
I've Learned …	85
I Was Just Saying …	86
Job Application	88
Laws Still In USA	90
Legal Wisdom	93
Lexophile Humour	97
Maid, The	99
Maintaining Your Insanity	100
Medical Records – US Doctors	101
Medical Records – Scottish NHS	102
Medical Terms	103
Men's Rules	104
Middle Wife	106
Military Conversations	108

Mother's Wisdom	110
My Pussy Quotes From Mrs Slocome	112
Newspaper Headlines	116
New Year's Email	117
Oneliners	118
Patent Brilliance	121
Politics Explained	122
Persistence	123
Pertinent Facts	126
Prayers For A New USA	127
Priest's Sermon Correction	129
Puns	130
Punning From Ireland	132
Quotes	134
Red Skelton On Happy Marriage	135
Religious Questions	136
School Exam Answers	138
Scientific Explanation	140
Senior's Bank Letter	141
Senior Health Care Plan	143
Sex Quotes	144
Smart Alec Answers	146
Sometimes …	148
Sydney Olympic Questions	149
Teacher Arrested	151
Terrorist Alerts Around The World	152
Toilet Rules	154
Travellers' Instructions	155
Unexpected Angels	158
Universal Wisdom	161
Unusual Body Finds	163
Woman's Wisdom	165
Word Meanings	166
Word Meanings - More	168
Wordplay	169
You Know When You're Living In 2018 When..	171
About the Author	172
Other books by Philip J Bradbury	174

Adam And Eve – the true story

Adam was hanging around the Garden of Eden feeling very lonely.
"What's wrong, Adam?" asked God.

Adam said he didn't have anyone to talk to.

God said that He was going to make Adam a companion and that it would be a woman.

God said, "This pretty lady will gather food for you, she will cook for you, and when you discover clothing, she will wash it for you. She will always agree with every decision you make and she will not nag you and will always be the first to admit she was wrong when you've had a disagreement. She will praise you! She will bear your children and never ask you to get up in the middle of the night to take care of them. She will NEVER have a headache and will freely give you love and passion whenever you need it."

"What will a woman like this cost?" asked Adam.

"An arm and a leg," said God.

"What can I get for a rib," asked Adam.

And the rest is history...

Adult Thoughts

- Raising teenagers is like nailing jelly to a tree.
- There is always a lot to be thankful for, if you take the time to look. For example, I'm sitting here thinking how nice it is that wrinkles don't hurt.
- One reason to smile is that every seven minutes of every day, someone in an aerobics class pulls a hamstring.
- Car sickness is the feeling you get when the monthly payment is due.
- The best way to keep kids at home is to make a pleasant atmosphere - and let the air out of their tyres.
- Families are like fudge . . . mostly sweet, with a few nuts.
- Today's mighty oak is just yesterday's nut that held its ground.
- Laughing helps. It's like jogging on the inside.
- Middle age is when you choose your cereal for the fibre, not the toy.
- My mind not only wanders; sometimes it leaves completely.
- If you can remain calm, you just don't have all the facts.

Advice Columns – why men shouldn't write them

Dear John,

I hope you can help me. The other day I set off for work, leaving my husband in the house watching TV. My car stalled and then it broke down about a mile down the road. I had to walk back home to get my husband's help. When I got home I couldn't believe my eyes – he was in our bedroom with our neighbour's daughter!

I am 32, my husband is 34 and the neighbour's daughter is 19. We have been married for 10 years. When I confronted him, he broke down and admitted they had been having an affair for the past six months. He won't go to counseling and I'm afraid I am a wreck and need advice urgently.

Can you please help?
Sincerely, Sheila.

Dear Sheila,

A car stalling after having been driven a short distance can be caused by a variety of faults with the engine. Start by checking that there is no debris in the fuel line. If it is clear, check the vacuum pipes and hoses on the intake manifold and also check the grounding wires. If none of these approaches solves the problem, it could be the fuel pump itself is faulty, causing low delivery pressure to the injectors.

I hope this helps.
John.

Age Concerns

- I learned that I like my teacher because she cries when we sing, *Silent Night*. Age 5
- I learned that our dog refuses to eat my broccoli too. Age 7
- I learned that when I wave to people in the country, they stop what they are doing and wave back. Age 9
- I learned that just when I get my room the way I like it, Mum makes me clean it up again. Age 12
- I learned that if you want to cheer yourself up, you should try cheering someone else up. Age 14
- I learned that although it is hard to admit it, I am secretly glad my parents are strict with me. Age 15
- I learned that silent company is often more healing than words of advice. Age 24
- I learned that brushing my child's hair is one of life's great pleasures. Age 26
- I learned that wherever I go, the world's worst drivers have followed me there. Drive carefully. Age 29
- I learned that if someone says something unkind about me, I must live so that no one will believe it. Age 30
- I learned that there are people who love you dearly but just have no idea of how to show it. Age 42
- I learned that you can make some one's day by simply sending them a little note. Age 44
- I learned that the greater a person's sense of guilt, the greater his or her need to cast blame on others. Age 46
- I learned that children and grandparents are natural allies. Age 47
- I learned that no matter what happens, or how bad it seems today, life does go on, and it will be better tomorrow. Age 48
- I learned that singing, *Amazing Grace* can lift my spirits for hours. Age 49
- I learned that motel mattresses are better on the side away from the phone. Age 50
- I learned that you can tell a lot about a man by the way he handles these three things: a rainy day, lost luggage, and tangled Christmas tree lights. Age 51

- I learned that keeping a vegetable garden is worth a medicine cabinet full of pills. Age 52
- I learned that regardless of your relationship with your parents, you miss them terribly after they die. Age 53
- I learned that making a living is not the same thing as making a life. Age 58
- I learned that if you want to do something positive for your children, work to keep, or improve your marriage. Age 61
- I learned that life sometimes gives you a second chance. Age 62
- I learned that you should never go through life with a catcher's mitt on both hands. You need to be able to throw something back. Age 64
- I learned that if you pursue contentment, it will elude you. But if you focus on your family, the needs of others, your work, meeting new people, and doing the very best you can, happiness will find you. Age 65
- I learned that whenever I decide something with kindness, I usually make the right decision. Age 66
- I have learned that if you don't do as your wife says, you will be in big trouble. Age 71
- I learned that everyone can use a prayer. Age 72
- I learned that even when I have pains, I do not have to be one. Age 82
- I learned that every day you should reach out and touch someone. People love that human touch - holding hands, a warm hug, or just a friendly pat on the back. Age 90
- I learned that I still have a lot to learn. Age 92

Age and Restaurants

A group of 40 year old golfing friends discuss where they should meet for dinner. Finally it is agreed that they should meet at the Ocean View restaurant because the waitresses there have low cut blouses and are pretty.

10 years later, at 50 years of age, the group again talks about where they should meet for dinner. Finally it is agreed that they should meet at the Ocean View restaurant because the food is very good and they have an excellent wine selection.

10 years later at 60 years of age, the group again discusses where they should meet. Finally it is agreed that they should meet at the Ocean View restaurant because they can eat there in peace and quiet and the restaurant has a beautiful view of the ocean.

10 years later, at 70 years of age, the group once again discusses where they should meet. Finally it is agreed that they should meet at the Ocean View restaurant because the restaurant is wheel chair accessible and they even have an elevator.

10 years later, at 80 years of age, the group once again talks about where they should meet for dinner. Finally it is agreed that they should meet at the Ocean View restaurant because they have never been there before.

Alphabet – Cockney

A for 'orses
B for mutton
C for yourself
D for dumb
E for brick
F for vessant
G for police
H yer guts
I for tower
J for orange
K for a cuppa'
L for leather
M for sis
N for a penny
O for the wall
P for a penny
Q for the movies
R for a mo'
S for you
T for two
U for mism
V for la France
W or quits
X for breakfast
Y for daughter
Z … can't remember this one!

Alzheimers Test

The following was developed as a mental age assessment by the School Psychiatry at Harvard University. Take your time and see if you can read each line aloud without a mistake. The average person over 40 years of age cannot do it!

This is this cat.
This is is cat.
This is how cat.
This is to cat.
This is keep cat.
This is an cat.
This is old cat.
This is fart cat.
This is busy cat.
This is for cat.
This is forty cat.
This is seconds cat.

Now go back and read the third word in each line from the top down.

Philip J Bradbury

Amish Anti-Ageing

A fifteen year old Amish boy and his father were in a mall. They were amazed by almost everything they saw but, especially, two shiny, silver walls that could move apart and then slide back together again.

The boy asked, "What is this Father?"

The father (never having seen an elevator) responded, "Son, I have never seen anything like this in my life, I don't know what it is."

While the boy and his father were watching with amazement, a fat old lady in a wheel chair moved up to the moving walls and pressed a button. The walls opened and the lady rolled between them into a small room. The walls closed and the boy and his father watched the small numbers above the walls light up sequentially. They continued to watch until it reached the last number. And then the numbers began to light up in the reverse order. Finally the walls opened up again and a gorgeous 24-year-old blond stepped out.

The father, not taking his eyes off the young woman, said quietly to his son, "Go get your Mother."

Aussie And The Emu

An Aussie truckie walks into an outback cafe with a full-grown emu behind him. The waitress asks them for their orders.

The truckie says, "A hamburger, chips and a coke," and turns to the emu, "What's yours?'

"Sounds great, I'll have the same," says the emu.

A short time later the waitress returns with the order. "That will be $9.40 please," she says.

The truckie reaches into his pocket and pulls out the exact change and pays.

The next day, the man and the emu come again and says, "A hamburger, chips and a coke."

The emu says, "Sounds great, I'll have the same."

Again the truckie reaches into his pocket and pays with exact change.

This becomes routine until the two enter again. "The usual?" asks the waitress.

"No, it's Friday night, so I'll have a steak, baked potato and a salad," says the man."

"Same for me," says the emu.

Shortly afterwards the waitress brings the order and says, "That will be $32.62."

Once again the man pulls the exact change out of his pocket and places it on the table.

The waitress can't hold back her curiosity any longer. "Excuse me mate, how do you manage to always pull the exact change from your pocket every time?"

"Well, love," says the truckie, "a few years ago, I was cleaning out the back shed and found an old lamp. When I cleaned it, a Genie appeared and offered me two wishes. My first wish was that if I ever had to pay for anything, I would just put my hand in my pocket and the right amount of money would always be there."

"That's brilliant!" says the waitress. "Most people would ask for a million dollars or something, but you'll always be as rich as you want, for as long as you live!"

"That's right. Whether it's a gallon of milk or a Rolls Royce, the exact money is always there." says the man.

Still curious the waitress asks, 'What's with the bloody emu?'

The truckie pauses, sighs, and answers, "My second wish was for a tall bird with a big arse and long legs, who agrees with everything I say."

Aviation Problems

After every flight, QANTAS pilots fill out a form known as a gripe sheet to tell mechanics about problems with the aircraft. The mechanics fix the problem and then document their repairs on the form. Here are some actual maintenance problems submitted by the pilots (marked with a 'P') and the solutions recorded by maintenance engineers (marked by an 'S'):

P: Left inside main tyre almost needs replacement.
S: Left inside main tyre almost replaced.

P: Test flight OK, auto-land very rough.
S: Auto-land not installed on this aircraft.

P: Something loose in cockpit.
S: Something tightened in cockpit.

P: Dead bugs on windshield.
S: Live bugs on back order.

P: Auto pilot in altitude-hold mode produces a 200 feet per minute descent.
S: Can't reproduce problem on the ground.

P: Evidence of leak on right main landing gear.
S: Evidence removed.

P: DME volume unbelievably loud.
S: DME volume set to more believable level.

P: Friction locks cause throttle levers to stick.
S: That's what friction locks are for.
P: IFF inoperative in OFF mode.
S: IFF always inoperative in OFF mode.

P: Suspect crack in windshield.
S: Suspect you're right.

Philip J Bradbury

P: Number 3 engine missing.
S: Engine found on right wing after brief search.

P: Aircraft handles funny.
S: Aircraft warned to straighten up, fly right and be serious.

P: Target radar hums.
S: Reprogrammed target radar with lyrics.

P: Mouse in cockpit.
S: Cat installed in cockpit.

P: Noise coming from under instrument panel. Sounds like a midget pounding on something with a hammer.
S: Took hammer away from midget.

Aviation Rules

From the Australian Aviation Magazine, June 2000:
- Every take-off is optional. Every landing is mandatory.
- If you push the stick forward, the houses get bigger. If you pull the stick back, they get smaller. That is, unless you keep pulling the stick all the way back, then they get bigger again.
- Flying isn't dangerous. Crashing is what's dangerous.
- It's always better to be down here wishing you were up there than up there wishing you were down here.
- The ONLY time you have too much fuel is when you're on fire.
- The propeller is just a big fan in front of the plane used to keep the pilot cool. When it stops, you can actually watch the pilot start sweating.
- When in doubt, hold on to your altitude. No one has ever collided with the sky.
- A 'good' landing is one from which you can walk away. A 'great' landing is one after which they can use the plane again.
- Learn from the mistakes of others. You won't live long enough to make all of them yourself.
- You know you've landed with the wheels up if it takes full power to taxi to the ramp.
- The probability of survival is inversely proportional to the angle of arrival. Large angle of arrival, small probability of survival and vice versa.
- Never let an aircraft take you somewhere your brain didn't get to five minutes earlier.

- Stay out of clouds. The silver lining everyone keeps talking about might be another airplane going in the opposite direction. Reliable sources also report that mountains have been known to hide out in clouds.
- Always try to keep the number of landings you make equal to the number of take offs you've made.
- There are three simple rules for making a smooth landing. Unfortunately no one knows what they are.
- You start with a bag full of luck and an empty bag of experience. The trick is to fill the bag of experience before you empty the bag of luck.
- Helicopters can't fly; they're just so ugly the earth repels them.
- If all you can see out of the window is ground that's going round and round and all you can hear is commotion coming from the passenger compartment, things are not at all as they should be.
- In the on-going battle between objects made of aluminium going hundreds of miles per hour and the ground going zero miles per hour, the ground has yet to lose.
- Good judgment comes from experience. Unfortunately, the experience usually comes from bad judgment.
- It's always a good idea to keep the pointy end going forward as much as possible.
- Keep looking around. There's always something you've missed.
- Remember, gravity is not just a good idea. It's the law. And it's not subject to repeal.
- The three most useless things to a pilot are the altitude above you, runway behind you, and a tenth of a second ago.

Beard Facts

- Science has shown that beards rarely sleep.
- Beards are almost completely immune to sarcasm.
- Beards quadruple handsomeness.
- Beards dramatically increase wood-chopping capability.
- Beards act as a homing beacon, attracting the jealousy and admiration of the beardless.
- Beards are a natural bear repellant when camping or wandering in the woods.
- Beards filter the air of toxins, pollution and stray food.
- Stroking of beard increases concentration and cognitive ability.
- Beards let you instinctually know where the nearest mountain is.
- Beards automatically fit your face.

Beneficiary Letters

Actual letters to the U.K. Department of Health:
- I want some repairs doing to my cooker as it backfired and burnt my knob off.
- I need money to buy special medicine for my husband as he is unable to masturbate his food.
- In accordance with your instructions I have given birth to twins in the enclosed envelope.
- I am sorry I forgot to put down all my childrens' names. This was due to contraceptional circumstances.
- I am very annoyed to find you have branded my son illiterate. This was a lie as I married his father a week before he was born.
- This is to let you know there is a smell coming from the man next door.
- Our lavatory seat is broken in half and is now in three pieces.

Billy Connoly Questions

I don't understand why …
- People point at their wrist while asking for the time. I know where my watch is – where's yours? Do I point at my crotch when I ask where the toilet is?
- People are willing to get off their bum to search the entire room for the TV remote because they refuse to walk to the TV and change the channel manually.
- People say 'Oh you just want to have your cake and eat it too'. Right! What good is a cake if you can't eat it?
- People say 'it's always the last place you look'. Of course it is. Why would you keep looking after you've found it?
- People say, while watching a film, 'did you see that?' No, I paid $12 to come to the cinema and stare at the floor!
- People ask 'Can I ask you a question?' Don't really give me a choice there, do you?
- When something is 'new and improved', which is it? If it's new, then there has never been anything before it. If it's an improvement, then there must have been something before it.
- People say 'life is short'. Life is the longest thing anyone ever does!! What can you do that's longer?
- When you are waiting for the bus, someone asks 'Has the bus come yet?' If the bus came would I be standing here?

Black Testicles

A male patient is lying in the hospital, wearing an oxygen mask over his mouth and nose, still heavily sedated from a difficult four-hour surgical procedure. A young student nurse arrives to give him a partial sponge bath.

"Nurse," he mumbles, from behind the mask, "are my testicles black?"

Embarrassed, the young nurse replies, "I don't know Sir. I'm only here to wash your upper body."

He struggles to ask again, "Nurse, are my testicles black?"

Concerned that he may elevate his vitals from worry about his testicles, she overcomes her embarrassment and sheepishly pulls back the covers. She raises his gown, holds his penis in one hand and his testicles in the other, lifting and moving them around and around gently. Then, she takes a close look and says, "No sir, they aren't and I assure you, there's nothing wrong with them, Sir."

The man pulls off his oxygen mask, smiles at her and says very slowly, "Thank you very much. That was wonderful, but listen very, very closely ... A r e - m y - t e s t - r e s u l t s - b a c k?"

Blondes

DEAD BMW

A blonde pushes her BMW into a gas station. She tells the mechanic it died. After he works on it for a few minutes, it is idling smoothly.

She asks, 'What's the story?'

He replies, 'Just crap in the carburettor.'

She asks, 'How often do I have to do that?'

SPEEDING TICKET

A police officer stops a blonde for speeding and asks her very nicely if he could see her license. She replied in a huff, 'I wish you guys would get your act together. Just yesterday you take away my license and then today you expect me to show it to you!'

EXPOSURE

A blonde is walking down the street with her blouse open and her right breast hanging out. A policeman approaches her and says, 'Ma'am, are you aware that I could cite you for indecent exposure?'

She asks, 'Why officer?'

'Because your breast is hanging out,' he says.

She looks down and says, 'OH MY GOD, I left the baby on the bus again!'

RIVER WALK

There's this blonde out for a walk. She comes to a river and sees another blonde on the opposite bank. 'Yoo-hoo!' she shouts, 'How can I get to the other side?'

The second blonde looks up the river then down the river and shouts back, 'You ARE on the other side.'

IN A VACUUM

A blonde was playing Trivial Pursuit one night. It was her turn. She rolled the dice and she landed on Science and Nature. Her question was, 'If you are in a vacuum and someone calls your name, can you hear it?'

She thought for a time and then asked, 'Is it on or off?'

KNITTING

A highway patrolman pulled alongside a speeding car on the freeway. Glancing at the car, he was astounded to see that the blonde behind the wheel was knitting! Realizing that she was oblivious to his flashing lights and siren, the trooper cranked down his window, turned on his bullhorn and yelled, 'PULL OVER!'

'NO!' the blonde yelled back, 'IT'S A SCARF!'

BLONDE ON THE SUN

A Russian, an American, and a Blonde were talking one day. The Russian said, 'We were the first in space!'

The American said, 'We were the first on the moon!'

The Blonde said, 'So what? We're going to be the first on the sun!'

The Russian and the American looked at each other and shook their heads. 'You can't land on the sun, you idiot! You'll burn up!' said the Russian.

To which the Blonde replied, 'We're not stupid, you know. We're going at night!'

DOGS

A girl was visiting her blonde friend, who had acquired two new dogs, and asked her what their names were. The blonde responded by saying that one was named Rolex and one was named Timex.

Her friend said, 'Whoever heard of someone naming dogs like that?'

'HelOOOooo,' answered the blond. 'They're watch dogs!'

Bureaucratic Wisdom

Dakota tribal wisdom says that when you discover you are riding a dead horse, the best strategy is to dismount. However, in business we often try other strategies with dead horses, including the following:
1. Buying a stronger whip.
2. Changing riders.
3. Saying things like. 'This is the way we have always ridden this horse.'
4. Appointing a committee to study the horse.
5. Arranging to visit other sites to see how they ride dead horses.
6. Creating a training session to increase our riding ability.
7. Changing the requirements so that we can declare, 'This horse is not really dead.'
8. Hiring contractors to ride the dead horse.
9. Harnessing several dead horses together for increased speed.
10. Declaring that, 'No horse is too dead to beat.'
11. Providing additional funding to increase the horse's performance.
12. Purchasing products to make dead horses run faster.
13. Declaring that the horse is, 'better, faster and cheaper' dead.
14. Forming a quality circle to find uses for dead horses.
15. Promoting the dead horse to a supervisory position.

It would be funnier if it weren't so true!!!!

California

You know you're in California when......
- Your co-worker has 8 body piercing and none are visible.
- You make over $300,000 and still can't afford a house.
- You take a bus and are shocked at two people carrying on a conversation in English.
- Your child's 3rd-grade teacher has purple hair, a nose ring, and is named Breeze.
- You can't remember ... is pot illegal?
- You've been to a baby shower that has two mothers and a sperm donor.
- You have a very strong opinion about where your coffee beans are grown, and you can taste the difference between Sumatran and Ethiopian.
- You know which restaurant serves the freshest arugula.
- You can't remember ... is pot illegal?
- A really great parking space can totally move you to tears.
- A low speed police pursuit will interrupt ANY TV broadcast.
- Gas costs $1.00 per gallon more than anywhere else in the US.
- A man gets on the bus in full leather regalia and crotchless chaps. You don't even notice.
- Unlike back home, the guy at 8:30am at Starbucks wearing the baseball cap and sunglasses who looks like George Clooney really IS George Clooney.
- Your car insurance costs as much as your house payment.
- Your hairdresser is straight, your plumber is gay, the woman who delivers your mail is into S&M, and your Mary Kay rep is a guy in drag.
- You can't remember ... is pot illegal?
- It's barely sprinkling rain and there's a report on every news station: 'STORM WATCH 2010.'
- You have to leave the big company meeting early because Billy Blanks himself is teaching the 4:00pm Tae Bo class.
- You pass an elementary school playground and the children are all busy with their cells or pagers.

- It's barely sprinkling rain outside, so you leave for work an hour early to avoid all the weather-related accidents.
- Hey! Is Pot Illegal????
- Both you AND your dog have therapists ....
- ... and the Terminator is your governor.

Childrens' Answers

Teacher: How old is your father?
Child: He is six years old.
Teacher: What? How is this possible?
Child: He became a father only when I was born.

Teacher: Maria, go to the map and find America.
Maria: Here it is.
Teacher: Correct. Now, class, who discovered America?
Class: Maria.

Teacher: Glenn, How do you spell crocodile?
Glenn: K-R-O-K-O-D-I-A-L
Teacher: No, that's wrong.
Glenn: Maybe it's wrong but you asked me how I spell it.

Teacher: Donald, what is the chemical formula for water?
Donald: H I J K L M N O
Teacher: What are you talking about?
Donald: Yesterday you said it was H to O.

Teacher: Clyde, your composition on My Dog is the same as your brother's. Did you copy his?
Clyde: No sir. It's the same dog.

Teacher: Harold, what do you call a person who keeps on talking when people are no longer interested?
Harold: A teacher.

Children's Fairy Story

The mind of a 6-year old is wonderful. First grade ... true story:

One day the first grade teacher was reading the story of the Three Little Pigs to her class. She came to the part of the story where the first pig was trying to accumulate the building materials for his home. She read, '... and so the pig went up to the man with the wheelbarrow full of straw and said, 'Pardon me sir, but may I have some of that straw to build my house?'' The teacher paused then asked the class, 'And what do you think that man said?'

One little boy raised his hand and said, 'I think he said, 'Holy crap! A talking pig!'' The teacher was unable to teach for the next 10 minutes.

And what an 11-year-old doesn't know ...

In a restaurant, a mother noticed her eleven-year-old daughter staring at a movie poster on the wall. The picture portrayed Superman standing in a phone booth.

The girl's mother whispered to her husband, "Doesn't she know who Superman is?"

He told her it was worse than that. "She doesn't know what a phone booth is."

Child Wisdom

- No matter how hard you try, you can't baptize cats.
- When your Mum is mad at your Dad, don't let her brush your hair.
- If your sister hits you, don't hit her back. They always catch the second person.
- Never ask your 3-year old brother to hold a tomato.
- Don't trust dogs to watch your food.
- Reading what people write on desks can teach you a lot.
- Don't sneeze when someone is cutting your hair.
- Puppies still have bad breath, even after eating a tic-tac.
- Never hold a Dust-Buster and a cat at the same time.
- School lunches stick to the wall.
- You can't hide a piece of broccoli in a glass of milk.
- Don't wear polka-dot underwear under white shorts.
- The best place to be when you're sad is Grandpa's lap.

Child Wisdom ... On Love

- Love is that first feeling you feel before all the bad stuff gets in the way.
- When my grandmother got arthritis, she couldn't bend over and paint her toenails anymore. So my grandfather does it for her all the time, even when his hands got arthritis too. That's love.
- When someone loves you, the way she says your name is different. You know that your name is safe in her mouth.
- Love is when a girl puts on perfume and a boy puts on shaving cologne and they go out and smell each other.
- Love is when you go out to eat and give somebody most of your French fries without making them give you any of theirs.
- Love is when someone hurts you. And you get so mad but you don't yell at him because you know it would hurt his feelings.
- Love is what makes you smile when you're tired.
- Love is when my mommy makes coffee for my daddy and she takes a sip before giving it to him, to make sure the taste is OK and it's not too hot.
- Love is when you kiss all the time. Then when you get tired of kissing, you still want to be together and you talk more. My mommy and daddy are like that. They look gross when they kiss but they look happy and sometimes they dance in the kitchen while kissing.
- Love is what's in the room with you at Christmas if you stop opening presents and listen.
- If you want to learn to love better, you should start with a friend who you hate.
- Love is hugging. Love is kissing. Love is saying no.
- When you tell someone something bad about yourself and you're scared she won't love you anymore. But then you get surprised because not only does she still love you, she loves you even more.
- There are 2 kinds of love. Our love. God's love. But God makes both kinds of them.
- Love is when you tell a guy you like his shirt, then he wears it every day.
- Love is like a little old woman and a little old man who are still friends even after they know each other so well.
- Love happened at my piano recital. I was on a stage and scared. I

looked at all the people watching me and saw my daddy waving and smiling. He was the only one doing that. I wasn't scared anymore.
- Love is if you hold hands and sit beside each other in the cafeteria. That means you're in love. Otherwise, you can sit across from each other and be okay.
- My mommy loves me more than anybody. You don't see anyone else kissing me to sleep at night.
- Love is when mommy gives daddy the best piece of chicken.
- Don't feel so bad if you don't have a boyfriend. There's lots of stuff you can do without one.
- Love is when mommy sees daddy smelly and sweaty and still says he is handsomer than Robert Redbird.
- If you want somebody to love you, then just be yourself. Some people try to act like somebody else the boy likes better. I think the boy isn't being very good if he does this to you and you should just find a nicer boy.
- Love is when your puppy licks your face even after you left him alone all day.
- Love is what makes people hide in the dark corners of movie theatres.
- Love goes on even when you stop breathing and you pick up where you left off when you reach heaven.
- I know my older sister loves me because she gives me all her old clothes and has to go out and buy new ones.
- You really shouldn't say 'I love you' unless you mean it. But if you mean it, you should say it a lot. People forget and need to be told.
- You have to fall in love before you get married. Then when you're married, you just sit around and read books together.
- I let my big sister pick on me because my Mom says she only picks on me because she loves me. So I pick on my baby sister because I love her.
- Love cards like Valentine's cards say stuff on them that we'd like to say ourselves, but we wouldn't be caught dead saying.
- When you love somebody, your eyelashes go up and down and little stars come out of you.
- Love means you never have to be lonely. There's always somebody to love, even if it's just a squirrel or a kitten.
- You can break love, but it won't die.

Child Wisdom ... On Religion

A little girl was talking to her teacher about whales. The teacher said it was physically impossible for a whale to swallow a human because even though it was a very large mammal its throat was very small. The little girl stated that Jonah was swallowed by a whale. Irritated, the teacher reiterated that a whale could not swallow a human; it was physically impossible.

The little girl said, "When I get to heaven I will ask Jonah".

The teacher asked, "What if Jonah went to hell?"

The little girl replied, "Then you ask him ".

A Kindergarten teacher was observing her classroom of children while they were drawing. She would occasionally walk around to see each child's work. As she got to one little girl who was working diligently, she asked what the drawing was.

The girl replied, "I'm drawing God."

The teacher paused and said, "But no one knows what God looks like."

Without missing a beat, or looking up from her drawing, the girl replied, "They will in a minute."

A Sunday school teacher was discussing the Ten Commandments with her five and six year olds. After explaining the commandment to "honour" thy Father and thy Mother, she asked, "Is there a commandment that teaches us how to treat our brothers and sisters?"

Without missing a beat one little boy answered, "Thou shall not kill."

One day a little girl was sitting and watching her mother do the dishes at the kitchen sink. She suddenly noticed that her mother had several strands of white hair sticking out in contrast on her brunette head. She looked at her mother and inquisitively asked, "Why are some of your hairs white, Mom?"

Her mother replied, "Well, every time that you do something wrong and make me cry or unhappy, one of my hairs turns white."

The little girl thought about this revelation for a while and then said, "Momma, how come ALL of grandma's hairs are white?"

The children had all been photographed, and the teacher was trying to persuade them each to buy a copy of the group picture. "Just think how nice it will be to look at it when you are all grown up and say, 'There's Jennifer, she's a lawyer,' or 'That's Michael, he's a doctor.'

A small voice at the back of the room rang out, "And there's the teacher, she's dead."

A teacher was giving a lesson on the circulation of the blood. Trying to make the matter clearer, she said, "Now, class, if I stood on my head, the blood, as you know, would run into it, and I would turn red in the face."

"Yes," the class said.

"Then why is it that while I am standing up right in the ordinary position the blood doesn't run into my feet?"

A little fellow shouted, "Cause your feet ain't empty."

The children were lined up in the cafeteria of a Catholic elementary school for lunch. At the head of the table was a large pile of apples. The nun made a note, and posted on the apple tray: "Take only ONE. God is watching." Moving further along the lunch line, at the other end of the table was a large pile of chocolate chip cookies. A child had written a note, "Take all you want. God is watching the apples."

The Sunday School teacher was describing how Lot's wife looked back and turned into a pillar of salt, when little Jason interrupted, "My Mommy looked back once, while she was driving," he announced triumphantly, "and she turned into a telephone pole!"

A Sunday school teacher was telling her class the story of the Good Samaritan. She asked the class, 'If you saw a person lying on the roadside, all wounded and bleeding, what would you do?'

A thoughtful little girl broke the hushed silence, 'I think I'd throw up.'

A Sunday school teacher asked, "Johnny, do you think Noah did a lot of fishing when he was on the Ark?"

"No," replied Johnny. "How could he, with just two worms."

The Meaning of Larf

A Sunday school teacher said to her children, "We have been learning how powerful kings and queens were in Bible times. But, there is a higher power. Can anybody tell me what it is?"

One child blurted out, "Aces!"

Nine-year-old Joey was asked by his mother what he had learned in Sunday School.

"Well, Mom, our teacher told us how God sent Moses behind enemy lines on a rescue mission to lead the Israelites out of Egypt. When he got to the Red Sea, he had his army build a pontoon bridge and all the people walked across safely. Then, he radioed headquarters for reinforcements. They sent bombers to blow up the bridge and all the Israelites were saved."

"Now, Joey, is that really what your teacher taught you?" his mother asked.

"Well, no, Mom. But, if I told it the way the teacher did, you'd never believe it!"

A Sunday School teacher decided to have her young class memorize one of the most quoted passages in the Bible; Psalm 23. She gave the youngsters a month to learn the chapter. Little Rick was excited about the task but, he just couldn't remember the Psalm. After much practice, he could barely get past the first line. On the day that the kids were scheduled to recite Psalm 23 in front of the congregation, Ricky was so nervous.

When it was his turn, he stepped up to the microphone and said proudly, "The Lord is my Shepherd, and that's all I need to know."

The preacher's five-year-old daughter noticed that her father always paused and bowed his head, for a moment, before starting his sermon. One day, she asked him why.

"Well, Honey," he began, proud that his daughter was so observant of his messages, "I'm asking the Lord to help me preach a good sermon."

"How come He doesn't do it?" she asked.

Philip J Bradbury

A rabbi said to a precocious six-year-old boy, "So your mother says your prayers for you each night? That's very commendable. What does she say?"

The little boy replied, "Thank God he's in bed!"

During the minister's prayer, one Sunday, there was a loud whistle from one of the back pews. Tommy's mother was horrified. She pinched him into silence and, after church, asked, "Tommy, whatever made you do such a thing?"

Tommy answered, soberly, "I asked God to teach me to whistle and He just then did!"

A pastor asked a little boy if he said his prayers every night.

"Yes, sir," the boy replied.

"And, do you always say them in the morning, too?" the pastor asked.

"No sir," the boy replied. "I ain't scared in the daytime."

When my daughter, Kelli, said her bedtime prayers, she would bless every family member, every friend, and every animal (current and past). For several weeks, after we had finished the nightly prayer, Kelli would say, 'And all girls.' As this soon became part of her nightly routine, to include this at the end, my curiosity got the best of me and I asked her, "Kelli, Why do you always add the part about all girls?"

Her response, "Because we always finish our prayers by saying 'All Men'!"

Little Johnny and his family were having Sunday dinner at his grandmother's house. Everyone was seated around the table as the food was being served. When Little Johnny received his plate, he started eating right away.

"Johnny! Please wait until we say our prayer." Said his mother

"I don't have to," The boy replied.

"Of course, you do," his mother insisted. "We say a prayer before eating, at our house."

"That's our house," Johnny explained. "But this is Grandma's house and she knows how to cook!"

Christmas Party Invitation

FROM: Patty Lewis, Human Resources Director
TO: All Employees
DATE: November 01, 2010
RE: Christmas Party

I'm happy to inform you that the company Christmas party will take place on December 23, starting at noon in the private function room at the grill house. There will be a cash bar and plenty of drinks! We'll have a small band playing traditional carols...feel free to sing along. And don't be surprised if our CEO shows up dressed as Santa Claus! A Christmas tree will be lit at 1:00pm. Exchange of gifts among employees can be done at that time; however, no gift should be over $10.00 to make the giving of gifts easy for everyone's pockets. This gathering is only for employees! Our CEO will make a special announcement at that time! Merry Christmas to you and your family.

Patty.

FROM: Patty Lewis, Human Resources Director
TO: All Employees
DATE: November 02, 2010
RE: Holiday Party

In no way was yesterday's memo intended to exclude our Jewish employees. We recognise that Chanukah is an important holiday, which often coincides with Christmas, though unfortunately not this year. However, from now on we're calling it our "Holiday Party". The same policy applies to any other employees who are not Christians or those still celebrating reconciliation day. There will be no Christmas tree present. No Christmas carols sung. We will have other types of music for your enjoyment. Happy now? Happy holidays to you and your family. Patty.

FROM: Patty Lewis, Human Resources Director
TO: All Employees
DATE: November 03, 2010
RE: Holiday Party

Regarding the note I received from a member of Alcoholics Anonymous requesting a non-drinking table.... you didn't sign your name. I'm happy to accommodate this request, but if I put a sign on a table that reads *AA only*, you wouldn't be anonymous anymore. How am I supposed to handle this? Somebody? Forget about the gifts exchange, no gifts exchange are allowed since the union members feel that $10.00 is too much money and executives believe $10.00 is a little too cheap. NO GIFTS EXCHANGE WILL BE ALLOWED.

FROM: Patty Lewis, Human Resources Director
TO: All Employees
DATE: November 04, 2010
RE: Holiday Party

What a diverse group we are! I had no idea that December 20 begins the Muslim holy month of Ramdan, which forbids eating and drinking during daylight hours. There goes the party! Seriously, we can appreciate how a luncheon at this time of year does not accommodate our Muslim employees' beliefs. Perhaps the Grill House can hold off on serving your meal until the end of the party, or else package everything for you to take it home in little foil doggy bags. Will that work? Meanwhile, I've arranged for members of Weight Watchers to sit farthest from the dessert buffet and pregnant women will get the table closest to the restrooms. Gays are allowed to sit with each other. Lesbians do not have to sit with gay men, each will have their own table. Yes, there will be a flower arrangement for the gay men's table. To the person asking permission to cross dress, no cross-dressing allowed. We will have booster seats for short people. Low-fat food will be available for those on a diet. We cannot control the salt used in the food so we suggest for those people with high blood pressure to taste first. There will be fresh fruits as dessert for Diabetics, the restaurant cannot supply "No Sugar" desserts. Sorry! Did I miss anything!?!?!?!
    Patty.

FROM: Patty Lewis, Human Resources Director
TO: All Employees
DATE: November 05, 2010
RE: The F%$king Holiday Party

Vegetarian pricks I've had it with you people!!! We're going to keep this party at the Grill House whether you like it or not, so you can sit quietly at the table furthest from the "grill of death", as you so quaintly put it, and you'll get your f%$king salad bar, including organic tomatoes. But you know, tomatoes have feelings too. They scream when you slice them. I've heard them scream! I'm hearing them scream right now!!! I hope you all have a rotten holiday! Drink, drive and die! The Bitch from HELL!!!!!!!!

FROM: Joan Bishop, Acting Human Resources Director
TO: All Employees
DATE: November 01, 20104
RE: Patty Lewis and Holiday Party

I'm sure I speak for all of us in wishing Patty Lewis a speedy recovery and I'll continue to forward your cards to her. In the meantime, management has decided to cancel our Holiday Party and give everyone the afternoon of the 23rd off with full pay. Happy Holidays!!

Classical Gaffes

Mrs. Gelegg had doubtless the glossiest and crispest brown curls in her drawers, as well as curls in various degrees of fuzzy laxness.
George Eliot, *The Mill on the Floss*

She touched his organ, and from that bright epoch even it, the old companion of his happiest hours, incapable as he had thought of elevation, began a new defined existence.
Charles Dickens, *Martin Chuzzelwit*

'Oh I can't explain,' cried Roderick impatiently, returning to his work, 'I've only one way of expressing my deepest feelings – It's this.' And he swung his tool.
Henry James, *Roderick Hudson*

Thus rendered bold by frequent intercourse, I dared to take her hand.
Edited by F. M. Reynolds, *The Keepsake*

Prince of the school, he had gained an easy dominion over the old Greek master by fascination of his parts.
Walter Pater, *Marius of Epicurean*

Mrs. Goddard was the mistress of the school ... where young ladies for enormous pay might be screwed out of health and into vanity.
Jane Austen, *Emma*

Sacred Poems and Private Ejaculation
George Herbert's subtitle to his famous book of poems, *The Temple*

Mrs. Ray declared that she had not found it at all hard and then, with laudable curiosity, seeing how little she knew about balls, desired to have an immediate account ...
Anthony Trollope, *Rachael Ray*

You think me a queer fellow already. It's not easy to tell you how I feel, not easy for so queer a fellow as I am to tell to in how many ways he's queer.
Henry James, *Passionate Pilgrim*

Computer Company Memo

This is a real memo sent out by a computer company to its field engineers, in all seriousness, about a computer peripheral problem. The author of this memo was quite genuine.

MEMO re: Replacement of Mouse Balls.

If a mouse fails to operate or should it perform erratically, it may need a ball replacement. Mouse balls are now available as FRU (Field Replacement Units). Because of the delicate nature of this procedure, replacement of mouse balls should only be attempted by properly trained personnel. Before proceeding, determine the type of mouse balls by examining the underside of the mouse. Domestic balls will be larger and harder than foreign balls. Ball removal procedures differ depending upon the manufacturer of the mouse. Foreign balls can be replaced using the pop-off method. Domestic balls are replaced by using the twist-off method. Mouse balls are not usually static sensitive. However, excessive handling can result in sudden discharge. Upon completion of ball replacement, the mouse may be used immediately. It is recommended that each person have a pair of spare balls for maintaining optimum customer satisfaction. Any customer missing his balls should contact the local personnel in charge of removing and replacing these necessary items. Please keep in mind that a customer without properly working balls is an unhappy customer.

Computer Dictionary For Kiwis (New Zealanders)

Monitor	Keeping an eye on the barbeque
Download	Get the firewood off the ute
Hard drive	Trip back home without any cold beer
Keyboard	Where you hang the ute and bike keys
Window	What you shut when it's cold
Screen	What you shut in the mosquito season
Byte	What mosquitoes do
Bit	What mosquitoes did
Mega Byte	What mosquitoes at the dam do
Chip	A bar snack
Micro Chip	What's left in the bag after you've eaten the chips
Modem	What you did to the lawns
Dot Matrix	Jim Matrix's wife
Laptop	Where the cat sleeps
Software	Plastic knives and forks you get at KFC
Hardware	Real stainless steel knives and forks from *The Warehouse*
Mouse	What eats the grain in the shed
Mouse Pad	Where the mouse takes the grain it does not eat
Mainframe	What holds the shed up
Web	What spiders make
Web Site	The shed (or under the verandah)
Cursor	The old bloke who swears a lot
Search Engine	What you do when the ute won't go
Yahoo	What you say when the ute does go
Upgrade	A steep hill
Server	The person at the pub who brings out the lunch
Mail Server	The bloke at the pub who brings out the lunch
User	The neighbour who keeps borrowing things
Network	When you have to repair your fishing net
Internet	Complicated fish net repair method
Netscape	When fish manoeuvres out of reach of net
Online	When you get the laundry hung out
Off Line	When the pegs don't hold the washing up

Consumer Labels

The intelligence of the human species has to be doubted when one reads the instructions that are deemed necessary on consumer products:
- On a blanket from Taiwan: Not to be used as protection from tornado.
- On a helmet-mounted mirror used by US cyclists: Remember, objects in the mirror are actually behind you.
- On a Taiwanese shampoo: Use repeatedly for severe damage.
- On the bottle-top of a (UK) flavoured milk drink: After opening, keep upright.
- On a New Zealand insect spray: This product not tested on animals.
- In a US guide to setting up a new computer: To avoid condensation forming, allow the boxes to warm up to room temperature before opening. (Sensible, but the instruction was INSIDE the box.)
- In some countries, on the bottom of Coke bottles: Open other end.
- On a Sears hairdryer: Do not use while sleeping.
- On a bag of Fritos: You could be a winner! No purchase necessary. Details inside. (The shoplifter special!)
- On a bar of Dial soap: Directions: Use like regular soap.
- On Tesco's Tiramisu dessert, printed on bottom of the Box: Do not turn upside down.
- On Marks & Spencer Bread Pudding: Product will be hot after heating.
- On a Korean kitchen knife: Warning: Keep out of children.
- On a string of Chinese-made Christmas lights: For indoor or outdoor

use only.
- On a Japanese food processor: Not to be used for the other use.
- On Sainsbury's peanuts: Warning - containing nuts.
- On an American Airlines packet of nuts: Instructions - Open packet, eat nuts.
- On a Swedish chainsaw: Do not attempt to stop chain with your hands or genitals.
- On a child's Superman costume: Wearing of this garment does not enable you to fly.
- On some frozen dinners: Serving suggestion: defrost.
- On a hotel-provided shower cap in a box: Fits one head.
- On packaging for a Rowenta iron: Do not iron clothes on body.
- On Nytol sleep aid: Warning - may cause drowsiness.

The American Dairy Association's huge success with the campaign 'Got Milk?' prompted them to expand their advertising to Mexico. It was soon brought to their attention that the Spanish translation read 'Are you lactating?'

When Parker Pen marketed a ball-point pen in Mexico, its ads were supposed to have read, 'It won't leak in your pocket and embarrass you'. The company thought that the word 'embarazar'' (to impregnate) meant to embarrass, so the ad read, 'It won't leak in your pocket and make you pregnant.'

The slogan for an American poultry producer, 'It takes a strong man to make a tender chicken' was translated into Spanish as 'It takes an aroused man to make a chicken affectionate.'

Corporate Capabilities

Chairman of the Board: Leaps tall buildings in a single bound, is more powerful than a locomotive, is faster than a speeding bullet, walks on water, talks with God.

President: Leaps short buildings in a single bound, is more powerful than a switch engine, is faster than a speeding BB, walks on water if the sea is calm, talks with God if special request is approved.

Executive Vice-President: Leaps short buildings with a running start and favourable winds, is almost as powerful as a switch engine, can fire a speeding bullet, walks on water in an indoor swimming pool, is occasionally addressed by God.

Vice President: Barely clears a Quonset hut, loses tug-of-war with a locomotive, can sometimes handle a gun without inflicting self-injury, swims well, talks to animals.

Manager: Makes high marks on the wall when trying to leap buildings, is run over by a locomotive, is not issued ammunition, dog paddles, talks to walls.

Supervisor: Runs into buildings, recognizes a locomotive two out of three times, wets himself with a water pistol, can't stay afloat without a life preserver, mumbles to himself

Secretary: Lifts buildings and walks under them, kicks locomotives off the tracks, catches speeding bullets in her teeth and eats them, freezes water with a single glance, she is God.

Cowboy Wisdom

- Don't squat with your spurs on.
- Don't interfere with something that ain't botherin' you none.
- Timing has a lot to do with the outcome of a rain dance.
- The easiest way to eat crow is while it's still warm. The colder it gets, the harder it is to swaller.
- If you find yourself in a hole, the first thing to do is to stop diggin'.
- If it don't seem like it's worth the effort, it probably ain't.
- It don't take a genius to spot a goat in a flock of sheep.
- The biggest troublemaker you'll probably ever have to deal with watches you shave his face in the mirror every morning.
- Never ask a barber if you need a haircut.
- Always drink upstream from the herd.
- 'Tis a whole lot easier riding the horse in the direction it's goin'.
- If you get to thinkin' you're a person of influence, try orderin' somebody else's dog around.
- Don't worry about bitin' off more 'n you can chew; your mouth is probably a whole lot bigger'n you think.
- Generally, you ain't learnin' nothing when your mouth's ajawin'.
- Tellin' a man to git lost and makin' him do it are two entirely different propositions.
- If you're ridin' ahead of the herd, take a look back every now and then to make sure it's still with ya.
- Good judgement comes from experience, and a lotta that comes from bad judgement.
- When you give a personal lesson in meanness to a critter or to a person, don't be surprised if they learn their lesson.
- When you're throwin' your weight around, be ready to have it thrown around by somebody else.
- Lettin' the cat out of the bag is a whole lot easier than puttin' it back.
- Always take a good look at what you're about to eat. It's not so important to know what it is, but it's sure crucial to know what it was.
- Never miss a good chance to shut up.
- The quickest way to double your money is to fold it over and put it back into your pocket.

- Always take your cigarettes outta your jeans pocket afore ya set on ya horse.
- If you keep your feet firmly on the ground, you'll have trouble putting on your pants!

Do You Know?

- Why doesn't Tarzan have a beard when he lives in the jungle without a razor?
- Why do we press harder on a remote control when we know the batteries are flat?
- Why do banks charge a fee on 'insufficient funds' when they know there is not enough?
- Why do Kamikaze pilots wear helmets?
- Why does someone believe you when you say there are four billion stars, but check when you say the paint is wet?
- Whose idea was it to put an 'S' in the word lisp?
- What is the speed of darkness?
- Why is it that people say they 'slept like a baby' when babies wake up every two hours?
- If the temperature is zero outside today and it's going to be twice as cold tomorrow, how cold will it be?
- Do married people live longer than single ones or does it only seem longer?
- How is it that we put man on the moon before we figured out it would be a good idea to put wheels on luggage?
- Why do people pay to go up tall buildings and then put money in binoculars to look at things on the ground?
- Who was the first person to say, 'See that chicken there - I'm going to eat the next thing that comes out of its bum.'?
- Why do toasters always have a setting so high that could burn the toast to a horrible crisp, which no decent human being would eat?

- Why is there a light in the fridge and not in the freezer?
- Why do people point to their wrist when asking for the time, but don't point to their bum when they ask where the bathroom is?
- Why does your gynecologist leave the room when you get undressed - they are going to look up there anyway!
- Why does Goofy stand erect while Pluto remains on all fours? They're both dogs!
- If quizzes are quizzical, what are tests?
- If corn oil is made from corn, and vegetable oil is made from vegetables, then what is baby oil made from?
- If electricity comes from electrons, does morality come from morons?
- Why do the Alphabet Song and Twinkle, Twinkle Little Star have the same tune?
- Did you ever notice that when you blow in a dog's face, he gets mad at you, but when you take him on a car ride, he sticks his head out the window?
- Does pushing the elevator button more than once make it arrive faster?

Discovery Of Radio

After having dug to a depth of 10 meters last year, British scientists found traces of copper wire dating back 100 years and came to the conclusion that their ancestors already had a telephone network more than 100 years ago.

Not to be outdone by the Brits, in the weeks that followed, Australian scientists dug to a depth of 20 meters, and shortly after, headlines in the Aussie newspapers read: "Australian archaeologists have found traces of 150 year old copper wire and have concluded that their ancestors already had an advanced high-tech communications network 50 years earlier than the Brits."

One week later, NZ Maori TV reported the following: "After digging as deep as 30 meters in his backyard in Te Kuiti, Hone Waiata, a King Country Kaumatua (Maori elder), reported that he found absolutely nothing. Hone has therefore concluded that 300 years ago Maori had already gone wireless."

Dog's Rules

- If I like it, it's mine.
- If it's in my mouth, it's mine.
- If I can take it from you, it's mine.
- If I had it a little while ago, it's mine.
- If it's mine, it must never appear to be yours in any way.
- If I'm chewing something up, all the pieces are mine.
- If it just looks like mine, it's mine.
- If I saw it first, it's mine.
- If you are playing with something and you put it down, it automatically becomes mine.
- If it's broken, it's yours.
- If you stare at someone long enough, eventually you'll get what you want.
- Don't go out without ID.
- If it's not wet and sloppy, it's not a kiss.
- Be aware of when to hold your tongue, and when to use it.
- Leave room in your schedule for a good nap.
- Always give people a friendly greeting.
- When you do something wrong, always take responsibility as soon as you're dragged out from under the bed.
- I will not play tug-of-war with Dad's underwear when he's on the toilet.
- The garbage collector is NOT stealing our stuff.
- I do not need to suddenly stand straight up when I'm lying under the coffee table.
- I will not roll my toys behind the fridge.
- I must shake the rainwater out of my fur BEFORE entering the house.
- I will not eat the cats' food, before or after they eat it.
- I will stop trying to find the few remaining pieces of clean carpet in the house when I am about to throw up.
- I will not roll on dead seagulls, fish, crabs, etc.
- 'Kitty box crunchies' are not food.
- I will not eat any more socks and then redeposit them in the backyard after processing.

- The diaper pail is not a cookie jar.
- I will not chew my human's toothbrush and not tell them.
- We do not have a doorbell. I will not bark each time I hear one on TV.
- I will not steal my mum's underwear and dance all over the backyard with it.
- My head does not belong in the refrigerator.
- I will not bite the officer's hand when he reaches in for Mum's driving licence and car registration.

How dogs and men are the same:
- Both take up too much space on the bed.
- Both have irrational fears about vacuum cleaning.
- Both mark their territory.
- Neither tells you what's bothering them.
- The smaller ones tend to be more nervous.
- Neither understands what you see in cats.
- Neither does any dishes.
- Both break wind shamelessly.
- Neither of them notices when you get your hair cut.
- Both like dominance games.
- Both are suspicious of the postman.

How dogs are better than men
- Dogs do not have problems expressing affection in public.
- Dogs miss you when you're gone.
- Dogs feel guilty when they've done something wrong.
- Dogs admit when they're jealous.
- Dogs are very direct about wanting to go out.
- Dogs do not play games with you - except fetch, and they never laugh at how you throw.
- You can train a dog.
- Dogs are easy to buy for.
- The worst social disease you can get from dogs is fleas.
- Dogs understand what 'no' means.
- Dogs mean it when they kiss you.

How dogs are better than women
- A dog's parents will never visit you.
- A dog loves you when you leave your clothes on the floor.
- A dog limits its time in the bathroom to a quick drink.
- A dog never expects you to telephone.
- A dog will not get mad at you if you forget its birthday.
- A dog does not care about the previous dogs in your life.
- A dog does not get mad at you if you pet another dog.
- A dog never expects flowers on Valentine's Day.
- The later you are, the happier a dog is to see you.
- A dog does not shop.

Donkey Types

What do you call a donkey with one leg?
A wonky donkey.

What do you call a donkey with one leg and one eye?
A winky wonky donkey.

What do you call a donkey with one leg, one eye and makin' love?
A bonky winky wonky donkey.

What do you call a donkey with one leg, one eye, makin' love while farting?
A stinky bonky winky wonky donkey.

What do you call a donkey with one leg, one eye, makin' love, farting and wearing blue suede shoes?
A honky tonky stinky bonky winky wonky donkey.

What do you call a donkey with one leg, one eye, makin' love, farting, wearing blue suede shoes and playing piano?
A plinky plonky honky tonky stinky bonky winky wonky donkey.

What do you call a donkey with one leg, one eye, makin' love, farting, wearing blue suede shoes, playing piano and driving a bus?
Very talented!

Dumb And Dumber

Recently, at McDonald's, I saw on the menu that you could have an order of 6, 9 or 12 chicken nuggets. I asked for a half-dozen.

'We don't have a half-dozen nuggets,' said the teenager at the counter.

'You don't?' I asked.

'We only have six, nine or twelve,' was the reply.

'So I can't order a half-dozen nuggets but I can order six?'

'That's right.'

I shook my head and ordered six.

Unbelievable but sadly true ... must have been the same one I asked for sweetener and she said they didn't have any, only Splenda and sugar.

I was checking out at the local ALDI Supermarket with just a few items and the lady behind me put her things on the belt close to mine. I picked up one of those dividers that they keep by the cash register and placed it between our things so they wouldn't get mixed.

After the girl had scanned all of my items, she picked up the divider, looking all over for the bar code so she could scan it. Not finding the bar code, she asked me. 'Do you know how much this is?'

I said, 'I've changed my mind. I don't think I'll buy that today.'

She said 'OK.' and I paid her for the things and left.

She had no clue to what had just happened. But the lady behind me had a big smirk on her face as I left.

Some years ago we had a work experience lass who was none too swift.

One day she was typing and turned to a secretary and asked, 'I'm almost out of typing paper. What do I do?'

'Just use paper from the photocopier', the secretary told her.

With that, the lass took her last remaining blank piece of paper, put it on the photocopier and proceeded to make five 'blank' copies.

A woman at work was seen putting a credit card into her computer disc drive and pulling it out very quickly.

When I inquired as to what she was doing, she said she was shopping on the internet and they kept asking for a credit card number, so she was using the ATM 'thingy.'

I recently saw a distraught young lady weeping beside her car.

'Do you need some help?' I asked.

She replied, 'I knew I should have replaced the battery to this remote door opener. Now I can't get into my car.'

Do you think they would have a battery to fit this?' she asked, pointing to a distant convenience store.

'Hmmm, I don't know. Do you have an alarm, too?' I asked.

'No, just this remote thingy,' she answered, handing it and the car keys to me.

When I took the keys and manually unlocked the door, I said to her, 'Why don't you drive over there and check about the batteries. It's a long walk....'

A mother called 000, very worried, asking the dispatcher if she needs to take her son to emergency, as he had eaten ants.

The dispatcher told her to give him some Benadryl and he should be fine.

The mother said, 'I just gave him some ant killer ...'

Dispatcher: 'Rush him in to emergency right now!'

Elder Wisdom I

- Growing old is mandatory; growing up is optional.
- Insanity is my only means of relaxation.
- Forget the health food. I need all the preservatives I can get.
- You know you're getting old when you stoop to tie your shoes and wonder what else you can do while you're down there.
- You're getting old when you get the same sensation from a rocking chair that you once got from a roller coaster.
- Perhaps you know why women over fifty don't have babies: They would put them down somewhere and forget where they left them.
- One of life's mysteries is how a two pound box of candy can make a person gain five pounds.
- Every time I think about exercise, I lie down till the thought goes away.
- God put me on earth to accomplish a certain number of things. Right now I am so far behind, I will live forever.
- It's frustrating when you know all the answers, but nobody bothers to ask you the questions.
- I finally got my head together, and my body fell apart.
- There cannot be a crisis this week; my schedule is already full.
- Time may be a great healer, but it's also a lousy beautician.
- The older you get, the tougher it is to lose weight, because by then your body and your fat are really good friends.
- Age doesn't always bring wisdom. Sometimes age comes alone.
- Just when I was getting used to yesterday, along came today.
- Sometimes I think I understand everything, then I regain consciousness.
- Amazing! You just hang something in your closet for a while, and it shrinks two sizes.
- It is bad to suppress laughter; it goes back down and spreads to your hips.
- Freedom of the press means no-iron clothes.
- Inside some of us is a thin person struggling to get out, but they can usually be sedated with a few pieces of chocolate cake.
- Lord, Keep your arm around my shoulder and your hand over my mouth ... AMEN!

The four stages of life
1. You believe in Santa Claus.
2. You don't believe in Santa Claus.
3. You are Santa Claus.
4. You look like Santa Claus.

And who looks after Father Christmas when he's ill?
The National Elf Service!

Some perks of being over 60
- Kidnappers are not very interested in you.
- In a hostage situation you are likely to be released first.
- No one expects you to run... anywhere.
- People call at 9pm and ask. "Did I wake you?"
- People no longer view you as a hypochondriac.
- There is nothing left to learn the hard way.
- Things you buy now won't wear out.
- You can eat supper at 5pm
- You can live without sex but not your glasses.
- You get into heated arguments about pension plans.
- You no longer think of speed limits as a challenge.
- You quit trying to hold your stomach in, no matter who walks into the room.
- You sing along with elevator music.
- Your eyes won't get much worse.
- Your investment in health insurance is finally beginning to pay off.
- Your joints are more accurate meteorologists than the national weather service.
- Your secrets are safe with your friends because they can't remember them either.
- Your supply of brain cells is finally down to a manageable size.
- You can't remember who sent you this list.
- And you notice these are all in big print for your convenience.

Elder Wisdom II

- Birds of a feather flock together . . . .and then shit on your car.
- A penny saved is a government oversight.
- The real art of conversation is not only to say the right thing at the right time, but also to leave unsaid the wrong thing at the tempting moment.
- The easiest way to find something lost around the house is to buy a replacement.
- He who hesitates is probably right.
- Did you ever notice: The Roman Numerals for forty (40) are XL.
- If you think there is good in everybody, you haven't met everybody.
- If you can smile when things go wrong, you have someone in mind to blame.
- The sole purpose of a child's middle name is so he can tell when he's really in trouble.
- There's always a lot to be thankful for if you take time to look for it. For example I am sitting here thinking how nice it is that wrinkles don't hurt.
- Did you ever notice: When you put the two words 'The' and 'IRS' together it spells 'Theirs...'
- Aging: Eventually you will reach a point when you stop lying about your age and start bragging about it.
- The older we get, the fewer things seem worth waiting in line for.
- Some people try to turn back their odometers. Not me, I want people to know 'why' I look this way. I've travelled a long way and some of the roads weren't paved.
- When you are dissatisfied and would like to go back to your youth, think of Algebra.
- You know you are getting old when everything either dries up or leaks.
- One of the many things no one tells you about ageing is that it is such a nice change from being young. Ah, being young is beautiful, but being old is comfortable.
- Long ago when men cursed and beat the ground with sticks, it was called witchcraft. Today, it's called golf.

Philip J Bradbury

Elder Q & A Forum

Q: Where can men over the age of 60 find younger, sexy women who are only interested in them and not just their money?
A: Try a bookstore, under fiction.

Q: What can a man do while his wife is going through menopause?
A: Keep busy. If you're handy with tools, you can finish the basement. When you're done you'll have a place to live.

Q: Someone has told me that menopause is mentioned in the bible. Is that true? Where can it be found?
A: Yes. Matthew 14:92: "And Mary rode Joseph's ass all the way to Egypt."

Q: How can you increase the heart rate of your 60-plus year old husband?
A: Tell him you're pregnant.

Q: How can you avoid that terrible curse of the elderly wrinkles?
A: Take off your glasses.

Q: Seriously! What can I do for these crow's feet and all those wrinkles on my face?
A: Go braless. It will usually pull them out.

Q: Why should 60-plus year old people use valet parking?
A: Valets don't forget where they park your car.

Q: Is it common for 60-plus year olds to have problems with short term memory storage?
A: Storing memory is not a problem. Retrieving it is the problem.

Q: As people age, do they sleep more soundly?
A: Yes, but usually in the afternoon.

Q: Where should 60-plus year olds look for eye glasses?
A: On their foreheads.

Q: What is the most common remark made by 60-plus year olds when they enter antique stores?
A: "Gosh, I remember these!"

Email Disclaimer

Yes, this is a real disclaimer – English lawyers are so pompous!!

This message (and any associated files) is intended only for the use of the individual or entity to which it is addressed and may contain information that is confidential, subject to copyright or constitutes a trade secret. If you are not the intended recipient you are hereby notified that any dissemination, copying or distribution of this message, or files associated with this message, is strictly prohibited and may be illegal. If you have received this message in error, please notify us immediately by replying to the message and deleting it from your computer. Messages sent to and from us may be monitored.

Internet communications cannot be guaranteed to be secure or error-free. Therefore, we do not accept responsibility for any errors or omissions that are present in this message, or any attachment, that have arisen as a result of e-mail transmission. Whilst we take reasonable precautions to ensure that e-mails sent by us are free from viruses we advise you to carry out your own virus checks. We make no representation or warranty as to the absence of viruses in this e-mail or any attachments and do not accept any liability for any damage, howsoever caused, by any virus that may be present in this e-mail. Any views or opinions presented are solely those of the author and do not necessarily represent those of the company. We do not accept any liability arising in any way from relying upon such views or opinions. Picture Finance Limited: Registered in England & Wales, Reg. Office c/o Morgan Cole, Bradley Court, Park Place, Cardiff, CF10 3DP, Reg. No. 5063897 COMPANY CONFIDENTIAL UNLESS STATED OTHERWISE.

Any opinions expressed in this message are those of the sender only and do not necessarily represent the views or opinions of FIRSTPLUS Financial Group or any associated companies. Registered Office: 54 Lombard Street, London, EC3P 3AH Registration Number: 3315543

The information contained in this message and any attachments is intended solely for the use of the individual or entity to whom it is addressed. It may contain privileged and confidential information and if you are not the intended recipient you must not copy, distribute or take action reliant on it. If you have received the e-mail in error please notify Administrator@FIRSTPLUS.CO.UK

This message has been checked for all known viruses by e:)scan.

An Alternative email disclaimer:

IMPORTANT: This email is intended for the use of the individual addressee(s) named above and may contain information that is confidential, privileged or unsuitable for overly sensitive persons with low self-esteem, no sense of humour or irrational religious beliefs. If you are not the intended recipient, any dissemination, distribution or copying of this email is not authorised (either explicitly or implicitly) and constitutes an irritating social faux pas. Unless the word absquatulation has been used in its correct context somewhere other than in this warning, it does not have any legal or grammatical use and may be ignored. No animals were harmed in the transmission of this email, although the kelpie next door is living on borrowed time, let me tell you. Those of you with an overwhelming fear of the unknown will be gratified to learn that there is no hidden message revealed by reading this warning backwards, so just ignore that Alert Notice from Microsoft.

However, by pouring a complete circle of salt around yourself and your computer you can ensure that no harm befalls you and your pets. If you have received this email in error, please add some nutmeg and egg whites, whisk and place in a warm oven for 40 minutes.

English Language Improvements

Now that you have an appreciation of absurdities of the English language, you won't be surprised to know that it is being 'corrected'.

The European Union commissioners have announced an agreement to adopt English as the preferred language for European communications. As part of negotiations, her Majesty's Government conceded that English spelling had room for improvement and has accepted a five-year plan for what will be known as *EuroEnglish*.

In the first year, 's' will be used instead of the soft 'c'. Sertainly, sivil servants will reseive this news with joy. Also, the hard 'c' will be replased with 'k'. Not only will this klear up konfusion, but typewriters kan have one less letter.

There will be growing publik enthusiasm in the sekond year, when the troublesome 'ph' will be replased by 'f', making words like 'fotograf' 20 per sent shorter.

In the third year, publik akseptanse of the new spelling kan be expekted to reach the stage where more komplikated changes are possible. Governments will enkourage the removal of double letters: always a deterent to akurate speling. Also, al wil agre that the horible mes of silent 'e's' in the languag is disgrasful, and they would go to.

By the folowing year, peopl wil be reseptiv to steps such as replasing 'th' by 'z' and 'w' by 'v'. During ze fifz year ze unesesary 'o' kan be dropd from vords kontaining 'ou' and similar changes vud of kors be aplid to ozer kombinations of leters. The furz year culd ned som car, to work.

After zis fifz year, ye vil hav a reli sensibl riten styl. Zer vil be no mor trubls or difikultis and evrivun vil find it ezi tu understand ech ozer. Ze filusofikal drem vil finali kum tru.

English Language Backwards

Olny srmat poelpe can raed tihs. I cdnuolt blveiee taht I cluod aulaclty uesdnatnrd waht I was rdanieg. The phaonmneal pweor of the hmuan mnid, aoccdrnig to a rscheearch at Cmabrigde Uinervtisy, it deosn't mttaer in waht oredr the ltteers in a wrod are, the olny iprmoatnt tihng is taht the frist and lsat ltteer be in the rghit pclae. The rset can be a taotl mses and you can sitll raed it wouthit a porbelm. Tihs is bcuseae the huamn mnid deos not raed ervey lteter by istlef, but the wrod as a wlohe. Amzanig huh? yaeh and I awlyas tghuhot slpeling was ipmorantt! if you can raed tihs psas it on !!

Fairy Tale For Men

Once upon a time, a Prince asked a beautiful Princess, "Will you marry me?"

The Princess said "NO!"

And the Prince lived happily ever after and rode motorcycles and went fishing and hunting and played golf and dated women half his age and drank beer and scotch and had tons of money in the bank and left the toilet seat up.

The end.

Famous Names In History

- The Frenchman who invented the cart? Monsieur Cartier.
- And his brother who invented maps so the carts didn't get lost? Cartographer Cartier.
- The boy who couldn't find his undies? They called him Nickerless.
- The great vegetable painter? Salador Dali.
- The very dangerous vicar? Parsonogen.
- Swine flu injection? A pig and a poke.
- The Ugly Duckling? Delusions of gander.

Finishing Things For Calm

I am passing this on to you because it definitely worked for me today and we could all do with some calm in our lives. Some doctor on TV this morning said the way to achieve inner peace was to finish all the things we had started. So I looked around my house to see the things I had started and not finished and, before I left for work, I finished off a bottle of Merlot, a bottle of Chardonnay, a bodle of Baileys, a pockage of Prungles, tha mainder of bot Prozac and Valium, remainda of chesecke an a box of chocletz. Yu haf no idr how bludy fablus I feel rite now. Plaese send dhis om to dem you fee ar in ned ov iennr pisss. An telum u fukin luvum!!

First Date

On Jay Leno's Tonight show, he went into the audience to find the most embarrassing first date that a woman ever had. This is the winner:

She said it was midwinter – snowing, quite cold and the guy had taken her skiing in the mountains outside Salt Lake City, Utah. It was a day trip (no overnight). They were strangers, after all, and had never met before. The outing was fun but relatively uneventful until they were headed home late that afternoon.

They were driving back down the mountain, when she gradually began to realize that she should not have had that extra latte. They were about an hour away from anywhere with a rest room and in the middle of nowhere! Her companion suggested she try to hold it, which she did for a while. Unfortunately, because of the heavy snow and slow going, there came a point where she told him that he had better stop and let her go beside the road, or it would be the front seat of his car.

They stopped and she quickly crawled out beside the car, yanked her pants down and started. In the deep snow she didn't have good footing, so she let her butt rest against the rear fender to steady herself.

Her companion stood on the side of the car watching for traffic and was a real gentleman who refrained from peeking. All she could think about was the relief she felt despite the rather embarrassing nature of the situation.

Upon finishing, however, she became aware of another sensation. As she bent to pull up her pants, she discovered her buttocks were firmly glued against the car's fender. Horrified by her plight and yet aware of the humour of the moment, she answered her date's concerns about "what is taking so long" with a reply that she was "freezing her butt off" and needed help!

He came around the car as she tried to cover herself with her sweater and then, as she looked imploringly into his eyes, he burst out laughing. She, too, got the giggles and when they finally managed to compose themselves, they assessed her dilemma. Obviously, as hysterical as the situation was, they also were faced with a real problem.

Both agreed it would take something hot to free her chilly cheeks from the grip of the icy metal! Thinking about what had gotten her into the predicament in the first place, both quickly realized that there was only one way to get her free. So, as she looked the other way, her first-time unzipped his pants and peed her butt off the fender.

Oh and how did the first date turn out? He became her husband and was sitting next to her on the Leno show.

Friendship Poem

Are you tired of all those mushy 'friendship' poems that always sound good but never actually come close to reality? Well, here is a friendship poem that really speaks to true friendship.

My Friend...

When you are sad, I will get you drunk and help you plot revenge against the sorry bastard who made you sad.

When you are blue, I'll try to dislodge whatever it is that is choking you.

When you smile, I'll know you FINALLY got laid.

When you are scared, I will rag you about it every chance I get.

When you are worried, I will tell you awful stories about how much worse it could be and tell you to quit whinging.

When you are confused, I will use small words to explain it to your dumb ass.

When you are sick, stay the hell away from me until you're well again. I don't want whatever you have.

When you are heaving, I will hold your hair while you pay homage to the porcelain god.

When you fall, I will piss myself laughing at you.

This is my oath, I pledge it till the end. Why, you may ask? Because you're my friend!

Forward this poem to ten of your closest friends and then get depressed when you realise you only have two friends and one of them is not speaking to you right now.

George W. Bush Wisdom

- If we don't succeed, we run the risk of failure.
- Republicans understand the importance of bondage between a mother and child.
- Welcome to Mrs Bush, and my fellow astronauts.
- Mars is essentially in the same orbit. Mars is somewhat the same distance from the Sun, which is very important. We have seen pictures where there are canals, we believe, and water. If there is water, that means there is oxygen. If oxygen, that means we can breathe.
- The Holocaust was an obscene period in our nation's history. I mean in this century's history. But we all lived in this century. 15/9/95
- I believe we are on an irreversible trend toward more freedom and democracy - but that could change. 22/5/98
- One word sums up probably the responsibility of any Governor, and that one word is 'to be prepared'. 6/12/93
- Verbosity leads to unclear, inarticulate things. 30/11/96
- I have made good judgments in the past. I have made good judgments in the future.
- The future will be better tomorrow.
- We're going to have the best educated American people in the world. 21/9/97
- People that are really very weird can get into sensitive positions and have a tremendous impact on history.
- I stand by all the misstatements that I've made. 17/8/93
- We have a firm commitment to NATO. We are a part of NATO. We have a firm commitment to Europe. We are a part of Europe.

- Public speaking is very easy.
- I am not part of the problem. I am a Republican.
- A low voter turnout is an indication of fewer people going to the polls.
- When I have been asked who caused the riots and the killing in LA, my answer has been direct and simple: Who is to blame for the riots? The rioters are to blame. Who is to blame for the killings? The killers are to blame.
- Illegitimacy is something we should talk about in terms of not having it. 20/5/96
- We are ready for any unforeseen event that may or may not occur. 22/9/97
- For NASA, space is still a high priority. 5/9/93
- Quite frankly, teachers are the only profession that teaches our children. 18/9/95
- The American people would not want to know of any misquotes that George Bush may or may not make.
- We're all capable of mistakes, but I do not care to enlighten you on the mistakes we may or may not have made.
- It isn't pollution that's harming the environment. It's the impurities in our air and water that are doing it.
- [It's] time for the human race to enter the solar system.

All this from the leader of the world's most powerful nation. By George, we're in good hands!

God's Children

Whenever your kids are out of control, you can take comfort from the thought that even God's omnipotence did not extend to God's kids …

After creating heaven and earth, God created Adam and Eve. And the first thing he said was: 'Don't.'

'Don't what?' Adam asked.

'Don't eat the forbidden fruit.' God said.

'Forbidden fruit? We got forbidden fruit? Hey, Eve...we got forbidden fruit!'

'No way!'

'Yes way!'

'Don't eat that fruit!' said God.

'Why?'

'Because I am your Father and I said so!' said God, wondering why he hadn't stopped after making the elephants. A few minutes later God saw his kids having an apple break and was angry.

'Didn't I tell you not to eat the fruit?' the First Parent asked.

'Uh huh,' Adam replied.

'Then why did you?'

'I dunno.' Eve answered.

'She started it!' Adam said.

'Did not!'

'Did too!'

'DID NOT!!'

Having had it with the two of them, God's punishment was that Adam and Eve should have children of their own. Thus, the pattern was set and it has never changed. But there is reassurance in this story. If you have persistently and lovingly tried to give them wisdom and they haven't taken it, don't be hard on yourself. If God had trouble handling children, what makes you think it would be a piece of cake for you?

Advice for the day: If you have a lot of tension and you get a headache, do what it says on the aspirin bottle: Take two and keep away from children.

God's Grass

GOD: Frank, you know all about gardens and nature. What in the world is going on down there on the planet? What happened to the dandelions, violets, milkweeds and stuff I started eons ago? I had a perfect no-maintenance garden plan. Those plants grow in any type of soil, withstand drought and multiply with abandon. The nectar from the long-lasting blossoms attracts butterflies, honey bees and flocks of songbirds. I expected to see a vast garden of colours by now. But, all I see are these green rectangles.

ST. FRANCIS: It's the tribes that settled there, Lord. The Suburbanites. They started calling your flowers 'weeds' and went to great lengths to kill them and replace them with grass

GOD: Grass? But it's so boring. It's not colourful. It doesn't attract butterflies, birds and bees; only grubs and earthworms. It's sensitive to temperatures. Do these Suburbanites really want all that grass growing there?

ST. FRANCIS: Apparently so, Lord. They go to great pains to grow it and keep it green. They begin each spring by fertilizing grass and poisoning any other plant that crops up in the lawn.

GOD: The spring rains and warm weather probably make grass grow really fast. That must make the Suburbanites happy.

ST. FRANCIS: Apparently not, Lord. As soon as it grows a little, they cut it ... sometimes, twice a week.

GOD: They cut it? Do they then bale it like hay?

ST. FRANCIS: Not exactly, Lord. Most of them rake it up and put it in bags.

GOD: They bag it? Why? Is it a cash crop? Do they sell it?

ST. FRANCIS: No Sir, just the opposite. They pay to throw it away.

GOD: Now, let me get this straight. They fertilize grass so it will grow. And, when it does grow, they cut it off and pay to throw it away?

ST. FRANCIS: Yes Sir.

GOD: These Suburbanites must be relieved in the summer when we cut back on the rain and turn up the heat. That surely slows the growth and saves them a lot of work.

ST. FRANCIS: You aren't going to believe this, Lord. When the grass stops growing so fast, they drag out hoses and pay more money to water it, so they can continue to mow it and pay to get rid of it.

GOD: What nonsense. At least they kept some of the trees. That was a sheer stroke of genius, if I do say so myself. The trees grow leaves in the spring to provide beauty and shade in the summer. In the autumn, they fall to the ground and form a natural blanket to keep moisture in the soil and protect the trees and bushes. It's a natural cycle of life.

ST. FRANCIS: You better sit down, Lord. The Suburbanites have drawn a new circle. As soon as the leaves fall, they rake them into great piles and pay to have them hauled away.

GOD: No!? What do they do to protect the shrub and tree roots in the winter to keep the soil moist and loose?

ST. FRANCIS: After throwing away the leaves, they go out and buy something which they call mulch. They haul it home and spread it around in place of the leaves.

GOD: And where do they get this mulch?

ST. FRANCIS: They cut down trees and grind them up to make the mulch.

GOD: Enough! I don't want to think about this anymore. St. Catherine, you're in charge of the arts. What movie have you scheduled for us tonight?

ST. CATHERINE: *Dumb and Dumber*, Lord. It's a story about...

GOD: Never mind, I think I just heard the whole story from St. Francis.

Hell Freezing Over

The following is an actual question given on a University of Washington chemistry mid-term. The answer by one student was so profound that the professor shared it with colleagues, via the internet:

Bonus Question: Is Hell exothermic (gives off heat) or endothermic (absorbs heat)?

Most of the students wrote proofs of their beliefs using Boyle's Law (gas cools when it expands and heats when it is compressed) or some variant.

One student, however, wrote the following:

First, we need to know how the mass of Hell is changing in time. So we need to know the rate at which souls are moving into Hell and the rate at which they are leaving.

I think that we can safely assume that once a soul gets to Hell, it will not leave. Therefore, no souls are leaving.

As for how many souls are entering Hell, let's look at the different religions that exist in the world today. Most of these religions state that if you are not a member of their religion, you will go to Hell. Since there is more than one of these religions and since people do not belong to more than one religion, we can project that all souls go to Hell.

With birth and death rates as they are, we can expect the number of souls in Hell to increase exponentially.

Now, we look at the rate of change of the volume in Hell because Boyle's Law states that in order for the temperature and pressure in Hell to stay the same, the volume of Hell has to expand proportionately as souls are added.

This gives two possibilities:

If Hell is expanding at a slower rate than the rate at which souls enter Hell, then the temperature and pressure in Hell will increase until all Hell breaks loose.

If Hell is expanding at a rate faster than the increase of souls in Hell, then the temperature and pressure will drop until Hell freezes over.

So which is it?

If we accept the postulate given to me by Teresa during my freshman year that, 'it will be a cold day in Hell before I sleep with you', and take into account the fact that I slept with her last night, then number 2 must be true, and thus I am sure that Hell is exothermic and has already frozen over.

The corollary of this theory is that since Hell has frozen over, it follows that it is not accepting any more souls and is therefore, extinct - leaving only Heaven thereby proving the existence of a divine being which explains why, last night, Teresa kept shouting 'Oh my God.'

THIS STUDENT RECEIVED THE ONLY 'A

Health Tips

Q: I've heard that cardiovascular exercise can prolong life. Is this true?
A: Your heart is only good for so many beats, and that's it ... don't waste them on exercise. Everything wears out eventually. Speeding up your heart will not make you live longer; that's like saying you can extend the life of your car by driving it faster. Want to live longer? Take a nap.

Q: Should I cut down on meat and eat more fruits and vegetables?
A: You must grasp logistical efficiencies. What does a cow eat? Hay and corn. And what are these? Vegetables. So a steak is nothing more than an efficient mechanism of delivering vegetables to your system. Need grain? Eat chicken. Beef is also a good source of field Grass (green leafy vegetable). And a pork chop can give you 100% of your recommended daily allowance of vegetable products.

Q: Should I reduce my alcohol intake?
A: No, not at all. Wine is made from fruit. Brandy is distilled wine. That means they take the water out of the fruity bit so you get even more of the goodness that way. Beer is also made out of grain.

Q: How can I calculate my body/fat ratio?
A: Well, if you have a body and you have body fat, your ratio is one to one. If you have two bodies, your ratio is two to one, etc.

Q: What are some of the advantages of participating in a regular exercise program?
A: Can't think of a single one, sorry. My philosophy is: No Pain ... Good

Q: Aren't fried foods bad for you?
A: YOU'RE NOT LISTENING!!! Foods are fried these days in vegetable oil. In fact, they're permeated in it. How could getting more vegetables be bad for you?

Q: Will sit-ups help prevent me from getting a little soft around the middle?
A: Definitely not! When you exercise a muscle, it gets bigger. You should only be doing sit-ups if you want a bigger stomach.

Q: Is chocolate bad for me?
A: Are you crazy? HELLO ...... Cocoa beans . another vegetable!!! It's the best feel-good food around!

Q: Is swimming good for your figure?
A: If swimming is good for your figure, explain whales to me.

Q: Is getting in-shape important for my lifestyle?
A: Hey! 'Round' is a shape!

I hope this has cleared up any misconceptions you may have had about food and diets and remember.......

Life should NOT be a journey to the grave with the intention of arriving safely in an attractive and well preserved body, but rather to skid in sideways - Chardonnay in one hand - strawberries in the other - body thoroughly used up, totally worn out, and screaming - WOO HOO!

Interesting And Useless Facts

- A Saudi Arabian woman can get a divorce if her husband doesn't give her coffee.
- A shark can detect one part of blood in 100 million parts of water.
- The 57 on a Heinz ketchup bottle represents the number of ingredients in the sauce.
- A rat can last longer without water than a camel.
- Your stomach has to produce a new layer of mucus every two weeks. Otherwise, it will digest itself.
- A raisin dropped in a glass of fresh champagne will bounce up and down continually from the bottom of the glass to the top.
- A male emperor moth can smell a female emperor moth up to 7 miles away.
- A giraffe can clean its ears with its 21-inch tongue!
- A female ferret will die if it goes into heat and cannot find a mate.
- 40% of McDonald's profits come from the sales of Happy Meals.
- Every person has a unique tongue print.
- During the chariot scene in Ben Hur a small red car can be seen in the distance.
- Einstein couldn't speak fluently until he was nine. His parents thought he might be retarded.
- On average, 12 new-borns will be given to the wrong parents daily.
- Chocolate kills dogs! True, chocolate effects a dog's heart and nervous system; a few ounces is enough to kill a small sized dog.
- Daniel Boone detested coonskin caps.
- Most lipstick contains fish scales.

- Donald Duck comics were banned from Finland because he doesn't wear pants.
- Ketchup was sold in the 1830s as medicine.
- Because metal was scarce, the Oscars given out during World War II were made of wood.
- Because of the shortage of glass, the first Volkswagen cars were built without rear windows.
- The number of possible ways of playing the first four moves per side in a game of chess is 318,979,564,000.
- There are no clocks in Las Vegas gambling casinos.
- There are no words in the dictionary that rhyme with: orange, purple, and silver!
- By raising your legs slowly and lying on your back, you can't sink in quicksand. P.S. do this before you sink below your waist.
- Cat's urine glows under a black light.
- Celery has negative calories! It takes more calories to eat a piece of celery than the celery has in it to begin with.
- Chewing gum while peeling onions will keep you from crying!
- An elephant can smell water three miles away.
- Guinness Book of Records holds the record for being the book most often stolen from Public Libraries.
- Babe Ruth wore a cabbage leaf under his cap to keep him cool! He changed it every 2 innings!
- A lion's roar can be heard from five miles away.
- Having blue eyes is actually a mutation. Before the mutation occurred, all humans had brown eyes.
- A Cryovolcano is a volcano that shoots out ice rather than lava. They can only exist in space and can be found on icy moons.
- Farmville players (on Facebook) outnumber real farmers in the US by a ratio of 60:1.
- Dr Seuss coined the word nerd.
- Dolly Parton once lost a Dolly Parton Look-a-like Contest.

I've Learned ...

- I've learned that no matter what happens, or how bad it seems today, life does go on, and it will be better tomorrow.
- I've learned that you can tell a lot about a person by the way he/she handles these three things:
  1. A rainy day,
  2. Lost luggage, and
  3. Tangled Christmas tree lights.
- I've learned that regardless of your relationship with your parents, you'll miss them when they're gone from your life.
- I've learned that making a 'living' is not the same thing as making a 'life.'
- I've learned that life sometimes gives you a second chance.
- I've learned that you shouldn't go through life with a catcher's mitt on both hands. You need to be able to throw something back.
- I've learned that if you pursue happiness, it will elude you. But if you focus on your family, your friends, the needs of others, your work and doing the very best you can, happiness will find you.
- I've learned that whenever I decide something with an open heart, I usually make the right decision.
- I've learned that even when I have pains, I don't have to be one.
- I've learned that every day you should reach out and touch someone. People love that human touch - holding hands, a warm hug, or just a friendly pat on the back.
- I've learned that I still have a lot to learn.
- I've learned that you should pass this on to someone you care about. I just did. Sometimes they just need a little something to make them smile.

Note:
People will forget what you said,
People will forget what you did, but
People will never forget how you made them feel.

I Was Just Saying ...

- I met this bloke with a didgeridoo and he was playing Dancing Queen on it. I thought, 'That's Aboriginal.'
- This lorry full of tortoises collided with a van full of terrapins. It was a turtle disaster.
- I told my girlfriend I had a job in a bowling alley. She said 'Tenpin?' I said, 'No, permanent.'
- I went in to a pet shop. I asked, 'Can I buy a goldfish?' The guy said, 'Do you want an aquarium?' I said, 'I don't care what star sign it is.'
- I was at a Garden Centre and I asked for something herby. They gave me a Volkswagen with no driver.
- I went to the local video shop and I said 'Can I borrow Batman Forever?' He said, 'No, you'll have to bring it back tomorrow'
- Batman came up to me and he hit me over the head with a vase and he went T'PAU! I said 'Don't you mean KAPOW??' He said 'No, I've got china in my hand.'
- I bought some Armageddon cheese today and it said on the packet, 'Best Before End'.
- I went to buy a watch, and the man in the shop said 'Analogue.' I said 'No, just a watch.'
- I went into a shop and asked, 'Can someone sell me a kettle?' The bloke said, 'Kenwood?' I said, 'Where is he then?'
- My mate is in love with two schoolbags. He's bisatchel.
- I said to the doctor, 'I'm frightened of lapels.' He said, 'You've got cholera.'
- I met the bloke who invented crosswords today. I can't remember his name, it's P something T something R.
- I was reading this book today, The History Of Glue. I couldn't put it down.
- I phoned the local ramblers club today, but the bloke who answered just went on and on.
- The recruitment consultant asked me 'What do you think of voluntary work?' I said 'I wouldn't do it if you paid me.'
- I was in the jungle and there was this monkey with a tin opener. I said, 'You don't need a tin opener to peel a banana.' He said, 'No, this is for the custard.'
- This policeman came up to me with a pencil and a piece of very thin

paper. He said, 'I want you to trace someone for me.'
- I told my mum that I'd opened a theatre. She said, 'Are you having me on?' I said, 'Well I'll give you an audition, but I'm not promising you anything.'
- I phoned the local builder today and asked him, 'Can I have a skip outside my house?' He said, 'I'm not stopping you!'
- This cowboy walks in to a German car showroom and he says 'Audi!'
- I fancied a game of darts with my mate. He said, 'Nearest the bull goes first' He went 'Baah' and I went 'Moo'. He said 'You're closest'
- I was driving up the motorway and my boss phoned me and he told me I'd been promoted. I was so shocked I swerved the car. He phoned me again to say I'd been promoted even higher and I swerved again. He then made me managing director and I went right off into a tree. The police came and asked me what had happened. I said 'I careered off the road.'
- I visited the offices of the RSPCA today. It's tiny: you couldn't swing a cat in there.
- I was stealing things in the supermarket today while balanced on the shoulders of a couple of vampires. I was charged with shoplifting on two counts.
- I bought a train ticket to France and the ticket seller asked 'Eurostar?' I said, 'Well I've been on telly but I'm no Robbie Williams.
- I phoned the local gym and I asked if they could teach me how to do the splits. He asked, 'How flexible are you?' I said, 'I can't make Tuesdays or Thursdays.'

Job Application

Job application a 17-year-old boy submitted at a McDonald's fast-food establishment in Florida:

NAME: Greg Bulmash

SEX: Not yet. Still waiting for the right person.

DESIRED POSITION: Company's President or Vice President. But seriously, whatever's available. If I was in a position to be picky, I wouldn't be applying here in the first place.

DESIRED SALARY: $185,000 a year plus stock options and a Michael Ovitz style severance package. If that's not possible, make an offer and we can haggle.

EDUCATION: Yes.

LAST POSITION HELD: Target for middle management hostility.

SALARY: Less than I'm worth.

MOST NOTABLE ACHIEVEMENT: My incredible collection of stolen pens and post-it notes.

REASON FOR LEAVING: It sucked.

HOURS AVAILABLE TO WORK: Any.

PREFERRED HOURS: 1:30-3:30 p.m., Monday, Tuesday, and Thursday.

DO YOU HAVE ANY SPECIAL SKILLS?: Yes, but they're better suited to a more intimate environment.

MAY WE CONTACT YOUR CURRENT EMPLOYER?: If I had one, I wouldn't be here would I?

DO YOU HAVE ANY PHYSICAL CONDITIONS THAT WOULD PROHIBIT YOU FROM LIFTING UP TO 50 LBS?: Of what?

DO YOU HAVE A CAR?: I think the more appropriate question here would be 'Do you have a car that runs?'

HAVE YOU RECEIVED ANY SPECIAL AWARDS OR RECOGNITION?: I may already be a winner of the Publishers Clearing House Sweepstakes.

DO YOU SMOKE?: On the job no, on my breaks yes.

WHAT WOULD YOU LIKE TO BE DOING IN FIVE YEARS?: Living in the Bahamas with a fabulously wealthy dumb sexy blonde super model who thinks I'm the greatest thing since sliced bread. Actually, I'd like to be doing that now.

DO YOU CERTIFY THAT THE ABOVE IS TRUE AND COMPLETE TO THE BEST OF YOUR KNOWLEDGE?
Yes. Absolutely.
SIGN HERE: Aries.

Laws Still In USA

Alabama
It is illegal to drive blindfolded and you can't drive the wrong way on a one way street if you have a lantern on the grill of your vehicle. If you go to church it is illegal to wear a fake moustache that causes laughter. You are not allowed to chain your alligator to a fire hydrant, keep an ice cream cone in your back pocket or flick boogers in the wind.

California
It is illegal to eat an orange in your bathtub, you are not allowed to prohibit children from playfully jumping over mud puddles and if you detonate a nuclear device in the city limits you will be fined $500.

Colorado
It is illegal for women to wear a red dress out on the streets after 7pm. You also cannot drive a black vehicle on Sunday in Denver.

Connecticut
It is illegal to walk across the street on your hands and, if you are bicycling, it is illegal to go over 65 miles per hour.

Florida
Women may be fined if they fall asleep under a hair dryer in a salon. It is illegal for a man to wear a strapless gown in public. You can't imitate an animal or sing in public wearing a swimsuit. It is illegal to fart in public on Thursdays after 6pm, have intercourse with a porcupine and women are not allowed to bungee jump naked before midday on Sunday or parachute if they are unmarried.

Georgia
If you have a giraffe it is illegal to tie it to a lamppost. You may not take a bath with orange peelings and if you live in Peachtree City, it is illegal to be homeless.

Illinois
It is illegal to eat in a restaurant that is on fire. You can't give whiskey to a dog or a cigar to any domesticated animal. You can't pee in your

neighbour's mouth or drink beer from a jug on the curb. If you want to go fishing you can't sit on a giraffe to do so. Humming in the streets, ice skating in the months of June and August, spitting on sidewalks and making faces at dogs are strictly prohibited. In some communities you can't install a basketball goal in your driveway and trucks must be parked in a closed garage.

Indiana
Bathing is illegal during the winter. You cannot attend any public function or ride in a street car if you have eaten garlic within 4 hours. It is illegal to make a monkey smoke a cigarette and men are not allowed to be urgent in public or to wink at a woman they don't know.

Kansas
It is illegal to put ice cream on a cherry pie, hunt for whales and stop at an intersection, get out of your car and fire three shots.

Kentucky
If you drink in Kentucky, you are considered sober unless you pass out. You can't shoot at game outside of your vehicle window, except for whales. If you are a married woman, you can't buy a hat without your husband's permission.

Louisiana
It is illegal to rob a bank and then shoot the teller with a water pistol. Biting someone with your natural teeth is "simple assault"; if you have false teeth it is "aggravated assault".

Maryland
It is illegal to swear outside the city limits of Baltimore and you can't throw hay out of a second story window.

Massachusetts
It is illegal to eat more than three sandwiches while at a wake. Snoring is prohibited unless all windows are shut and locked. If you have a goatee, it is illegal unless you have purchased a license to have one. It is illegal to put tomatoes in chowder, and you can't crap on your neighbor.

Michigan
It is illegal for a woman to cut her hair unless she has her husband's permission. It's illegal to be mean to women and children and you cannot kill a dog using a decompression chamber. Couples are banned from sex in an automobile unless it is parked on their own property, you can't scowl at your wife on Sunday and you can't willfully destroy your old radio. It is illegal to let your pig run free unless it has ring in its nose. It is illegal to paint sparrows and sale them as parakeets. You cannot serenade your girlfriend and all bathing suits must be approved by the Head of Police, and you can't smoke while in bed.
It is illegal to have sex unless it is in the missionary position, drive a red car on Sundays or have more than two forms of state-issued identification. You can't stand next to a building unless you have a reason for being there and anyone entering or allowing someone to enter a massage parlour after 11 pm will be charged with a misdemeanor.

Nebraska
It is illegal for a parent to allow a child to burp in church.

Legal Wisdom

As recently reported in the Massachusetts Bar Association Lawyers Journal, the following are 22 questions which were actually asked of witnesses by attorneys during trials and, in certain cases, the responses given by insightful witnesses:

1. 'Now doctor, isn't it true that when a person dies in his sleep, he doesn't know about it until the next morning?'
2. 'The youngest son, the twenty-year old, how old is he?'
3. 'Were you present when your picture was taken?'
4. 'Were you alone or by yourself?'
5. 'Was it you or your younger brother who was killed in the war?'
6. 'Did he kill you?'
7. 'How far apart were the vehicles at the time of the collision?'
8. 'You were there until the time you left, is that true?'
9. 'How many times have you committed suicide?'
10. Q: 'So the date of conception (of the baby) was August 8th?'
    A: 'Yes.'
    Q: 'And what were you doing at that time?'
11. Q: 'She had three children, right?'
    A: 'Yes.'
    Q: 'How many were boys?'
    A: 'None.'
    Q: 'Were there any girls?'
12. Q: 'You say the stairs went down to the basement?'
    A: 'Yes.'
    Q: 'And these stairs, did they go up also?'
13. Q: 'Mr. Slattery, you went on a rather elaborate honeymoon, didn't you?'
    A: 'I went to Europe, Sir.'
    Q: 'And you took your new wife?'
14. Q: 'How was your first marriage terminated?'
    A: 'By death.'
    Q: 'And by whose death was it terminated?'
15. Q: 'Can you describe the individual?'
    A: 'He was about medium height and had a beard.'
    Q: 'Was this a male, or a female?'

16. Q: 'Is your appearance here this morning pursuant to a deposition notice which I sent to your attorney?'
    A: 'No, this is how I dress when I go to work.'
17. Q: 'Doctor, how many autopsies have you performed on dead people?'
    A: 'All my autopsies are performed on dead people.'
18. Q: 'All your responses must be oral, OK? What school did you go to?'
    A: 'Oral.'
19. Q: 'Do you recall the time that you examined the body?'
    A: 'The autopsy started around 8:30 p.m.'
    Q: 'And Mr. Dennington was dead at the time?'
    A: 'No, he was sitting on the table wondering why I was doing an autopsy.'
20. Q: 'You were not shot in the fracas?'
    A: 'No, I was shot midway between the fracas and the navel.'
21. Q: 'Are you qualified to give a urine sample?'
    A: 'I have been since early childhood.'
22. Q: What was the first thing your husband said to you that morning?
    A: He said, 'Where am I, Cathy?'
    Q: And why did that upset you?
    A: My name is Susan!

And some others from around the world ...

23. Q: Do you know if your daughter has ever been involved in voodoo?
    A: We both do.
    Q: Voodoo?
    A: We do.
    Q: You do?
    A: Yes, voodoo.
24. Q: What gear were you in at the moment of the impact?
    A: Gucci sweats and Reeboks.
25. Q: Now doctor, isn't it true that when a person dies in his sleep, he doesn't know about it until the next morning?
    A: Did you actually pass the bar exam?
26. Q: Are you sexually active?
    A: No, I just lie there.

27. Q: This myasthenia gravis, does it affect your memory at all?
    A: Yes.
    Q: And in what ways does it affect your memory?
    A: I forget.
    Q: You forget? Can you give us an example of something you forgot?
28. Q: The youngest son, the twenty-year-old, how old is he?
    A: He's twenty, much like your IQ.
29. Q: Were you present when your picture was taken?
    A: Are you sh **** ng me?
30. Q: So the date of conception (of the baby) was August 8th?
    A: Yes.
    Q: And what were you doing at that time?
    A: Getting laid
31. Q: She had three children, right?
    A: Yes.
    Q: How many were boys?
    A: None.
    Q: Were there any girls?
    A: Your Honor, I think I need a different attorney. Can I get a new attorney?
32. Q: How was your first marriage terminated?
    A: By death.
    Q: And by whose death was it terminated?
    A: Take a guess.
33. Q: Can you describe the individual?
    A: He was about medium height and had a beard.
    Q: Was this a male or a female?
    A: Unless the circus was in town, I'm going with male.
34. Q: Is your appearance here this morning pursuant to a deposition notice which I sent to your attorney?
    A: No, this is how I dress when I go to work.
35. Q: Doctor, how many of your autopsies have you performed on dead people?
    A: All of them. The live ones put up too much of a fight.
36. Q: Do you recall the time that you examined the body?
    A: The autopsy started around 8:30 p.m.
    Q: And Mr. Denton was dead at the time?

A: If not, he was by the time I finished.
38. Q: Are you qualified to give a urine sample?
    A: Are you qualified to ask that question?
39. Q: Doctor, before you performed the autopsy, did you check for a pulse?
    A: No.
    Q: Did you check for blood pressure?
    A: No.
    Q: Did you check for breathing?
    A: No.
    Q: So, then it is possible that the patient was alive when you began the autopsy?
    A: No.
    Q: How can you be so sure, Doctor?
    A: Because his brain was sitting on my desk in a jar.
    Q: I see, but could the patient have still been alive, nevertheless.
    A: Yes, it is possible that he could have been alive and practicing law.

Lexophile Humour

- I wondered why the baseball was getting bigger. Then it hit me.
- Police were called to a daycare where a three-year-old was resisting a rest.
- Did you hear about the guy whose whole left side was cut off? He's all right now.
- The roundest knight at King Arthur's round table was Sir Cumference.
- The butcher backed up into the meat grinder and got a little behind in his work.
- To write with a broken pencil is pointless.
- When fish are in schools they sometimes take debate.
- The short fortune-teller who escaped from prison was a small medium at large.
- A thief who stole a calendar got twelve months.
- A thief fell and broke his leg in wet cement. He became a hardened criminal.
- Thieves who steal corn from a garden could be charged with stalking.
- We'll never run out of math teachers because they always multiply.
- When the smog lifts in Los Angeles, U.C.L.A.
- The professor discovered that her theory of earthquakes was on shaky ground.
- The dead batteries were given out free of charge.
- If you take a laptop computer for a run you could jog your memory.
- A dentist and a manicurist fought tooth and nail.
- A bicycle can't stand alone; it is two tired.
- A will is a dead giveaway.
- A chicken crossing the road: poultry in motion.
- If you don't pay your exorcist you can get repossessed.
- Show me a piano falling down a mine shaft and I'll show you A-flat miner.
- When a clock is hungry it goes back four seconds.
- The guy who fell onto an upholstery machine has fully recovered.
- You are stuck with your debt if you can't budge it.
- Local Area Network in Australia: The LAN down under.

- He broke into song because he couldn't find the key.
- A calendar's days are numbered.
- A lot of money is tainted: 'Taint yours, and 'taint mine.
- A boiled egg is hard to beat.
- He had a photographic memory which was never developed.
- Those who get too big for their britches will be exposed in the end.
- If you jump off a Paris bridge, you are in Seine.
- When she saw her first strands of grey hair, she thought she'd dye.
- Bakers trade bread recipes on a knead to know basis.
- Santa's helpers are subordinate clauses.
- Acupuncture: a jab well done.

Maid, The

The maid asked for a pay increase. The wife was very upset about this and decided to talk to her about the raise. She asked: 'Now Maria, why do you want a pay increase?'

Maria: 'Well, Señora, there are tree reasons why I wan an increase. The first is that I iron better than you.'

Wife: 'Who said you iron better than me?'

Maria: 'Jor husband say so.'

Wife: 'Oh.'

Maria: 'The second reason is that I am a better cook than you.'

Wife: 'Nonsense, who said you were a better cook than me?'

Maria: 'Jor husband did.'

Wife: 'Oh.'

Maria: 'The third reason is that I am better at sex than you in bed.'

Wife: (really furious now) 'Did my husband say that as well?'

Maria: 'No Señora ... the gardener did.'

Wife: 'So how much do you want?'

Maintaining Your Insanity

Ways to maintain a healthy level of insanity:
- At lunch time, sit in your parked car with sunglasses on and point a hair dryer at passing cars. See if they slow down.
- Page yourself over the intercom. Don't disguise your voice.
- Every time someone asks you to do something, ask if they want fries with that.
- Put your garbage can on your desk and label it "in."
- Put decaf in the coffee maker for three weeks. Once everyone has gotten over their caffeine addictions, switch to espresso.
- In the memo field of all your cheques, write "For smuggling diamonds."
- Finish all your sentences with "In accordance with the prophecy."
- Don't use any punctuation.
- As often as possible, skip rather than walk.
- Order a diet water whenever you go out to eat, with a serious face.
- Specify that your drive-through order is "to go."
- Sing along at the opera.
- Go to a poetry recital and ask why the poems don't rhyme?
- Put mosquito netting around your work area and play tropical sounds all day.
- Five days in advance, tell your friends you can't attend their party because you're not in the mood.
- Have your co-workers address you by your wrestling name, Rock Bottom.
- When the money comes out of the ATM, scream "I won! I Won!"
- When leaving the zoo, start running towards the parking lot, yelling "Run for your lives, they're loose!!"
- Tell your children over dinner, "Due to the economy, we are going to have to let one of you go."

Medical Records – US Doctors

- Patient has chest pain if she lies on her left side for over a year.
- She has had no rigors or shaking chills, but her husband states she was hot in bed last night.
- The patient is tearful and crying constantly. She also appears to be depressed.
- Discharge status: Alive but without permission.
- Healthy appearing decrepit 69-year-old male, mentally alert but forgetful.
- The patient refused an autopsy.
- Patient has left his white blood cells at another hospital.
- The patient had waffles for breakfast and anorexia for lunch.
- She is numb from her toes down.
- While in the ER, she was examined, X-rated and sent home.
- The skin was moist and dry.
- Occasional, constant, infrequent headaches.
- Patient was alert and unresponsive.
- She stated that she had been constipated for most of her life until 1995 when she got a divorce.
- I saw your patient today, who is still under our car for physical therapy.
- Exam of genitalia reveals that he is circus sized.
- The lab test indicated abnormal lover function.
- The patient was to have a bowel resection. However, he took a job as a stockbroker instead.
- Skin: Somewhat pale but present.
- The pelvic examination will be done later on the floor.
- Patient was seen in consultation by Dr. Blank, who felt we should sit on the abdomen and I agree.
- Large brown stool ambulating in the hall.
- Patient has two teenage children but no other abnormalities.

Medical Records – Scottish NHS

- The patient was in his usual state of good health until his airplane ran out of fuel and crashed.
- Between you and me we ought to be able to get this woman pregnant.
- The patient has no previous history of suicides.
- The patient refused an autopsy.
- I saw your patient today, who is still under our car for physical therapy.
- Skin: somewhat pale, but present.
- By the time he was admitted, his rapid heart had stopped, and he was feeling better.
- On the second day the knee was better and on the third day it had disappeared completely.
- Discharge status: alive but without my permission
- Patient's medical history has been remarkably insignificant with only a 40Ib weight gain in the past 3 days.
- Rectal examination revealed a normal-sized thyroid.
- The patient has been depressed since she began seeing me in 1993.
- She slipped on the ice and apparently her legs went in separate directions in early December.

Medical Terms

Artery	The study of paintings
Bacteria	Back door of a cafeteria
Barium	What the doctors do when the patients die
Bowel	A letter like A, E, I, O or U
Caesarian section	A neighbourhood in Rome
Cat scan	Searching for kitty
Cauterise	Made eye contact with her
Coma	A punctuation mark
D. & C.	Where Washington is
Dilate	To live longer
Enema	Not a friend
Fester	A small lie
Genital	Not a Jew
G. I. series	A soldiers ball game
Hangnail	Coat hook
Impotent	Distinguished, well known
Labour pain	Getting hurt at work
Medical staff	Doctor's cane
Morbid	A higher offer
Nitrates	Cheaper than day rates
Node	'Was aware of'
Outpatient	A person who has fainted
Pap smear	A fatherhood test
Pelvis	A cousin to Elvis
Recovery room	Place to do upholstery
Rectum	Dang near killed 'em
Secretion	Hiding something
Seizure	Roman emperor
Tablet	A small table
Terminal illness	Getting sick at the airport
Tumour	More than one
Urine	Opposite of 'you're out'
Varicose	Nearby

Philip J Bradbury

Men's Rules

We always hear 'the rules' from the female side. Now here are the rules from the male side. These are our rules! Please note – these are all numbered '1' ON PURPOSE!

1 Learn to work the toilet seat. You're a big girl. If it's up, put it down. We need it up, you need it down. You don't hear us complaining about you leaving it down.
1 Sunday sports. It's like the full moon or the changing of the tides. Let it be.
1 Shopping is NOT a sport. And no, we are never going to think of it that way.
1 Crying is blackmail.
1 Ask for what you want. Let us be clear on this one: Subtle hints do not work! Strong hints do not work! Obvious hints do not work! Just say it!
1 Yes and No are perfectly acceptable answers to almost every question.
1 Come to us with a problem only if you want help solving it. That's what we do. Sympathy is what your girlfriends are for.
1 Anything we said 6 months ago is inadmissible in an argument. In fact, all comments become null and void after 7 days.
1 If you think you're fat, you probably are. Don't ask us.
1 If something we said can be interpreted two ways and one of the ways makes you sad or angry, we meant the other one.
1 You can either ask us to do something or tell us how you want it done. Not both. If you already know best how to do it, just do it yourself.
1 Whenever possible, please say whatever you have to say during commercials.
1 Christopher Columbus did not need directions and neither do we.
1 ALL men see in only 16 colours, like Windows default settings. Peach, for example, is a fruit, not a colour. Pumpkin is a vegetable, not a colour. We have no idea what mauve is.
1 If it itches, it will be scratched. We do that.
1 If we ask what is wrong and you say 'nothing,' we will act like

nothing's wrong. We know you are lying, but it is just not worth the hassle.
- If you ask a question you don't want an answer to, expect an answer you don't want to hear.
- When we have to go somewhere, absolutely anything you wear is fine ... really.
- Don't ask us what we're thinking about unless you are prepared to discuss such topics as baseball, the shotgun formation, or monster trucks.
- You have enough clothes.
- You have too many shoes.
- I am in shape. Round is a shape.
- Thank you for reading this. Yes, I know, I have to sleep on the couch tonight; but did you know men really don't mind that? It's like camping.

How Scottish men deal with emotions

Jock and his girlfriend were watching a TV show about psychology, dealing with the subject of mixed emotions.

He turned to her and said, "This is utter crap, there's nothing you could tell me that would make me happy and sad at the same time."

With her eyes firmly focused on the TV screen she said, "Out of all your mates, you've got the biggest willy."

Middle Wife

By an Anonymous 2nd grade teacher

I've been teaching now for about fifteen years. I have two kids myself, but the best birth story I know is the one I saw in my own second grade classroom a few years back.

When I was a kid, I loved show-and-tell so I always have a few sessions with my students. It helps them get over shyness and usually, show-and-tell is pretty tame. Kids bring in pet turtles, model airplanes, pictures of fish they catch, stuff like that. And I never, ever place any boundaries or limitations on them. If they want to lug it in to school and talk about it, they're welcome.

Well, one day this little girl, Erica, a very bright, very outgoing kid, takes her turn and waddles up to the front of the class with a pillow stuffed under her sweater. She holds up a snapshot of an infant.

"This is Luke, my baby brother, and I'm going to tell you about his birthday. First, Mom and Dad made him as a symbol of their love, and then Dad put a seed in my Mom's stomach and Luke grew in there. He ate for nine months, through an umbrella cord."

She's standing there with her hands on the pillow and I'm trying not to laugh and wishing I had my camcorder with me. The kids are watching her in amazement.

"Then, about two Saturdays ago, my Mom starts saying and going, 'Oh, Oh, Oh, Oh!'" Erica puts a hand behind her back and groans. "She walked around the house for, like an hour, 'Oh, oh, oh!'" (Now this kid is doing a hysterical duck walk and groaning.)

"My Dad called the middle wife. She delivers babies, but she doesn't have a sign on the car like the Domino's man. They got my Mom to lie down in bed like this." (Then Erica lies down with her back against the wall.)

"And then, pop! My Mom had this bag of water she kept in there in case he got thirsty, and it just blew up and spilled all over the bed, like psshhheew!" (This kid has her legs spread with her little hands mimicking water flowing away. It was too much!)

"Then the middle wife starts saying 'push, push,' and 'breathe, breathe'. They started counting, but never even got past ten. Then, all of a sudden, out comes my brother. He was covered in yucky stuff that they all said it was from Mom's play-center, (placenta) so there must be a lot of toys inside there. When he got out, the middle wife spanked him for crawling up in there."

Then Erica stood up, took a big theatrical bow and returned to her seat. I'm sure I applauded the loudest. Ever since then, when it's show-and-tell day, I bring my camcorder, just in case another 'Middle Wife' comes along.

Military Conversations

An actual radio conversation between a US naval ship and Canadian authorities off the coast of Newfoundland in October 1995. The Radio conversation was released by the Chief of Naval Operations on Oct. 10, 1995.

US Ship: Please divert your course 0.5 degrees to the south to avoid a collision.

CND reply: Recommend you divert your course 15 degrees to the South to avoid a collision.

US Ship: This is the Captain of a US Navy Ship. I say again, divert your course.

CND reply: No. I say again, you divert YOUR course!

US Ship: THIS IS THE AIRCRAFT CARRIER USS CORAL SEA, WE ARE A LARGE WARSHIP OF THE US NAVY. DIVERT YOUR COURSE NOW!!

CND reply: This is a lighthouse ... your call.

And we rely on these people to defend us!!!

National Public Radio interview between a female broadcaster and US Army General Reinwald who was about to sponsor a Boy Scout Troop visiting his military installation.

FEMALE INTERVIEWER: 'So, General Reinwald, what things are you going to teach these young boys when they visit your base?'

GENERAL REINWALD: 'We're going to teach them climbing, canoeing, archery, and shooting.'

FEMALE INTERVIEWER: Shooting! That's a bit irresponsible isn't it?'

GENERAL REINWALD: 'I don't see why, they'll be properly supervised on the rifle range.'

FEMALE INTERVIEWER: 'Don't you admit that this is a terribly dangerous activity to be teaching children?'

GENERAL REINWALD: 'I don't see how,....we will be teaching them proper rifle range discipline before they even touch a firearm.'

FEMALE INTERVIEWER: 'But you're equipping them to become violent killers.'

GENERAL REINWALD: 'Well, you're equipped to be a prostitute, but you're not one, are you?'

The radio went silent and the interview ended.

Mother's Wisdom

The following came from an anonymous Mother in Austin, Texas – *Things I've learned from my Children*:
- A king size waterbed holds enough water to fill a 2000 sq. ft. house 4 inches deep.
- If you spray hair spray on dust bunnies and run over them with roller blades, they can ignite.
- A 3-year old voice is louder than 200 adults in a crowded restaurant.
- If you hook a dog leash over a ceiling fan, the motor is not strong enough to rotate a 42 pound boy wearing Batman underwear and a Superman cape. It is strong enough, however, if tied to a paint can, to spread paint on all four walls of a 20x20 ft. room.
- You should not throw baseballs up when the ceiling fan is on. When using a ceiling fan as a bat, you have to throw the ball up a few times before you get a hit. A ceiling fan can hit a baseball a long way.
- The glass in windows (even double-pane) doesn't stop a baseball hit by a ceiling fan.
- When you hear the toilet flush and the words 'uh oh,' it's already too late.
- Brake fluid mixed with Clorox makes smoke, and lots of it.
- A six-year old can start a fire with a flint rock even though a 36-year old man says they can only do it in the movies.
- Certain Legos will pass through the digestive tract of a 4-year old.
- Play dough and microwave should not be used in the same sentence.
- Super glue is forever.

- No matter how much Jell-O you put in a swimming pool you still can't walk on water.
- Pool filters do not like Jell-O.
- VCR's do not eject PB&J sandwiches even though TV commercials show they do.
- Garbage bags do not make good parachutes.
- Marbles in gas tanks make lots of noise when driving.
- You probably do not want to know what that odour is.
- Always look in the oven before you turn it on; plastic toys do not like ovens.
- The fire department in Austin, Texas, has a 5-minute response time.
- The spin cycle on the washing machine does not make earthworms dizzy. It will, however, make cats dizzy.
- Cats throw up twice their body weight when dizzy.

P.S. 60% of men who read this will try mixing Clorox and brake fluid.

My Pussy Quotes From Mrs Slocome

From the British TV series, *Are You Being Served?*

Our Figures are Slipping - "It's very short notice - there's my pussy to consider. Who's going to let it out?"

Cold Comfort - "You're lucky to have me at all, Captain Peacock. I had to thaw me pussy out before I came. It had been out all night."

The Think Tank - "Well, if I'm not home on the stroke of six, my pussy goes mad."

Hoorah for the Holidays - "Oh, Mr. Rumbold, I hope this isn't going to take long. My pussy's been locked up for eight hours."

The Hand of Fate - "You know, animals are very psychic. I mean, the least sign of danger and my pussy's hair stands on end."

German Week - "You know, this sort of thing just isn't fair on my pussy. She has a go at the furniture if I'm not there prompt."

New Look - "It's a wonder I'm here at all, you know. My pussy got soakin' wet. I had to dry it out in front of the fire before I left."

Christmas Crackers - "I hope we're not going to be late tonight. Because I've left Winston clinging to the curtain ring - he refuses to come down. The mere sight of my pussy drives him mad."

No Sale - "Having a bath at 6 o'clock in the morning played havoc with my pussy."

Forward, Mr Grainger - "Well, speaking personally, I never have any trouble getting up in the morning. My pussy's just like an alarm clock. Every morning at 6:15 it drops its clockwork mouse on my pillow."

Fire Practice - "Can we get on with it? I can't bear the sight of my pussy, standing at the door with a tin-opener in its mouth."

Fire Practice - "Oh, I don't need a fire alarm. At the first sign of smoke, my pussy rushes into the garden and it sits on the concrete tortoise in the middle of the goldfish bowl."

The Father Christmas Affair - "Well, I hope it's not going to take long. If I'm not home on the stroke of seven, my pussy starts clawing at my busy lizzy."

Mrs Slocombe Expects - "Well, the central heating broke down. I had to light the oven and hold my pussy in front."

A Change is as Good as a Rest - "But they're all dogs! Is there no demand for mechanical pussies?"

The Old Order Changes - "I hope this isn't going to take long, Captain Peacock. The last time I was late, a fireman had to climb out of my bedroom window and risk his life on a narrow ledge tryin' to grab hold of my pussy."

Goodbye, Mr. Grainger - "Oh, look! It's a diamante collar for my pussy."

The Club - "Well, if I'm to spend an evening in this club, there'll have to be accommodation for my pussy."

Shedding the Load - "She went right up to the sergeant at the desk, and she said, 'Have any of your constables reported having seen this lady's pussy?'"

A Bliss Girl - "What about this fog? My pussy's been gasping all night."

Happy Returns - "Well, I can't stay too late. The man next door is popping in every half-hour to keep an eye on my pussy."

The Junior - "I've got to get home. If my pussy isn't attended to by 8 o'clock, I shall be strokin' it for the rest of the evening."

The Apartment - "Well, you know how clumsy those removal men are. I'm not havin' 'em handlin' my pussy."

Philip J Bradbury

The Apartment - "Mr Humphries! Leave my pussy alone!"

The Hero - "Today's the day my pussy comes of age!"

Anything You Can Do - "If there are any leftovers, my pussy gobbles them up in a flash."

Is It Catching? - "But at 7 o'clock tonight, my pussy's expectin' to see a friendly face."

Closed Circuit - "Is that Mr Ackbar? Mrs Slocombe here, your next-door neighbour. I wonder, would you do me a favour? Would you go to my front door, bend down, and look through the letter-box? And if you can see my pussy, would you drop a sardine on the mat?"

Roots? - "I've got a sculptor coming this evening. He's going to do my pussy in clay."

Roots? - "It's at a very critical stage. All last night, I had to keep it on the table covered by a wet flannel. And tonight at 9 o'clock, all the neighbors are comin' in to watch him pour plaster of paris all over it... and then put it in a very hot oven."

Sweet Smell of Success - "I inadvertently dropped some on my pussy, and there were tomcats throwin' themselves against my cat-flap all night."

Calling All Customers - "I ought to ring my neighbor and ask her to look in on my pussy."

Calling All Customers - "They're for my pussy...d'you know, it wins a prize every time I show it."

Monkey Business - "But then they spotted my pussy and we're off."

Lost and Found - "I suddenly realized he means more to me than anything else in the world...except my pussy, of course."

Goodbye, Mrs Slocombe - "Twenty minutes later my pussy was in a basket on its way to Scotland."

The Night Club - "Look, I'm trying to get my pussy on the phone!"

Friends and Neighbours - "My only problem is, will my pussy feel at home in a strange place?"

Grace & Favour #1 - "Mr Humphries, would you hold my pussy while I alight?"

Grace & Favour #1 - "Somebody help me, please! That naughty goat has got hold of my pussy and won't let go!"

Grace & Favour #2 - "He won't be so confident when he sees my pussy."

Grace & Favour #2 - "They're not having my pussy! And I am unanimous in that!"

Grace & Favour #5 - "I'll put my pussy in front of the hole, and the next time he comes out, he'll get a nasty shock."

Grace & Favour #5 - "Captain Peacock, have you seen my pussy?"

Grace & Favour #7 - "My pussy was very agitated."

Grace & Favour #9 -- "He was devoted to me...and to the pussy I had at the time."

Grace & Favour #10 - "I've never seen one of those before...a two hundred year-old pussy."

Grace & Favour #10 - "I have a pussy of great antiquity, and I'd like him to take a look at it."

Grace & Favour #11 - "He'd have raised a pussy."

Grace & Favour #12 - "Do you know, I found my pussy trapped in my drawers."

Newspaper Headlines

The NZ Herald's 25 Best Newspaper Headlines of 1999. Just remember most of you people take your news source from writers like these. It's a scary thought really.

- Something Went Wrong in Jet Crash, Experts Say
- Include Your Children When Baking Cookies
- Police Begin Campaign to Run Down Jaywalkers
- Drunks Get Nine Months in Violin Case
- Iraqi Head Seeks Arms.
- Is There a Ring of Debris around Uranus?
- Prostitutes Appeal to Pope
- Panda Mating Fails; Veterinarian Takes Over
- British Left Waffles on Falkland Islands
- Teacher Strike Idles Kids
- Clinton Wins Budget; More Lies Ahead
- Plane Too Close to Ground, Crash Probe Told
- Miners Refuse to Work After Death
- Juvenile Court to Try Shooting Defendant
- Stolen Painting Found by Tree
- Local High School Dropouts Cut in Half
- War Dims Hope for Peace
- If Strike Isn't Settled Quickly, It May Last a While
- Man Struck by Lightning Faces Battery Charge
- New Study of Obesity Looks for Larger Test Group
- Astronaut Takes Blame for Gas in Space
- Kids Make Nutritious Snacks
- Two Sisters Reunited after 18 Years in Checkout Counter
- Typhoon Rips Through Cemetery; Hundreds Dead
- Cold wave linked to temperatures
- Enfield (London) Couple Slain; Police Suspect Homicide
- Red Tape Holds Up New Bridges
- Hospitals are Sued by 7 Foot Doctors

New Year's Email

With the New Year almost upon us, I'd like to extend my heartfelt appreciation to all of you who have taken the time and trouble to send me "forwards" over the past 12 months. Thank you for making me feel safe, secure, blessed and healthy.

Extra thanks to whoever sent me the email about rat crap in the glue on envelopes - cause I now have to go get a wet towel every time I need to seal an envelope.

Also, I scrub the top of every can I open for the same reason.

Because of your genuine concern, I no longer drink Coca Cola because I know it can remove toilet stains, which is not exactly an appealing characteristic.

I no longer check the coin return on pay phones because I could be pricked with a needle infected with AIDS.

I no longer use cancer-causing deodorants even though I smell like a water buffalo on a hot day.

I no longer go to shopping centres because someone might drug me with a cologne sample and rob me.

I no longer eat KFC because their "chickens" are actually horrible mutant freaks with no eyes or feathers.

I no longer worry about my soul because at last count, I have 363,214 angels looking out for me.

I have learned that God only answers my prayers if I forward an e-mail to seven of my friends and make a wish within five minutes.

I no longer have any savings because I gave it to a sick girl on the internet who is about to die in the hospital (for the 1,387,258th time).

I no longer have any money at all in fact - but that will change once receive the $15,000 that Microsoft and AOL are sending me for participating in their special on-line email program.

Yes, I want to thank you all so much for looking out for me that I will now return the favour!

If you don't send this e-mail to at least 144,000 people in the next 7 minutes, a large pigeon with a wicked case of diahorrea will land on your head at 5:00PM (EST) this afternoon. I know this will occur because it actually happened to a friend of my next door neighbour's ex-mother-in-law's second husband's cousin's beautician.

HAPPY NEW YEAR anyway.

Philip J Bradbury

Oneliners

- Legalize maru... mara... moua... mawo... ummm... pot.
- I went to school to become a wit, but I only got halfway through.
- Kentucky: Five million people. Fifteen last names.
- How do you get a tissue to dance? Put a little boogie in it.
- It takes money to make money because you have to copy the design exactly.
- It's easy to identify people who can't count to ten. They're in front of you in the supermarket express lane.
- My check engine light came on the other day. I popped the hood and looked, and the engine is STILL there! Silly light ...
- I drank a whole bottle of bug repellent by mistake the other day... Now my fly won't close.
- I can explain it to you, but I can't understand it for you.
- Around the office, they call him God. He's rarely seen, holier than thou, and if he does anything it's considered a bloody miracle.
- My whole life, I've been slow and passed it off as meticulous.
- Pack your bags, it's time to go on a guilt trip.
- The way some people find fault, you would think there's some kind of reward.
- I wonder how long I would be on *Hold* if my call wasn't important to them?
- I've got a bad feeling about the 21st Century. I feel better about the 20th. I made it through alive in that one.
- I am not going bald. I'm getting more head.
- I think that your magnetic personality has wiped the data strip in your brain clean.
- I dialled a 900 number to get some financial advice. They advised me to quit calling 900 numbers.
- If the universe is expanding, why can't find a parking space?
- Refuse Novocain...Transcend Dental Medication.
- My ex-wife said she will dance on my grave. I have now arranged to be buried at sea.
- What does it mean when a naked man is in your bed gasping for breath and calling your name? You didn't hold the pillow down long enough.

- Are part time band leaders semi-conductors?
- Is it time for your medication or mine?
- I just did a background check. It's still right behind me.
- If a case of the clap spreads, is it called applause?
- I like your approach. Now let's see your departure.
- If God meant me to be naked, He would have made my skin fit better.
- Of course men can multitask - they read on the toilet.
- Just heard the psychic hotline had to shut down due to budget cuts. Wonder if they saw that coming...
- I am a light eater. As soon as it gets light I start eating.
- My neighbour knocked on my door at 2:30am this morning. Can you believe that ... 2:30am?! Luckily for him I was still up playing my bagpipes.
- The Grim Reaper came for me last night and I beat him off with a vacuum cleaner. Talk about Dyson with death!
- I sat on the train this morning opposite a stunning Thai girl. I kept thinking to myself, please don't get an erection, please don't get an erection ... but she did.
- Man calls 999 and says, "I think my wife is dead". The operator asks, "how do you know?" He says, "The sex is the same but the ironing is building up!"
- I was in bed with a blind girl last night and she said that I had the biggest p*nis she had ever laid her hands on. I said, "You're pulling my leg".
- I saw a poor old lady fall over today on the ice!! At least I presume she was poor - she only had $1.20 in her purse.
- My girlfriend thinks that I'm a stalker. Well, she's not exactly my girlfriend yet.
- I woke up last night to find the ghost of Gloria Gaynor standing at the foot of my bed. At first I was afraid ... then I was petrified.
- The wife has been missing a week now. Police said to prepare for the worst. So I have been to the charity shop to get all her clothes back.
- A mate of mine recently admitted to being addicted to brake fluid. When I quizzed him on it he reckoned he could stop any time...
- I went to the cemetery yesterday to lay some flowers on a grave. As I was standing there I noticed 4 grave diggers walking about with a coffin. 3 hours later and they're still walking about with it. I thought

to myself, they've lost the plot!!
- My daughter asked me for a pet spider for her birthday, so I went to our local pet shop and they were $70! Blow this, I thought, I can get one cheaper off the web.
- Statistically, 6 out of 7 dwarves are not happy.
- I went around to a friend's house today. His wife was there with their new-born baby. She asked if I'd like to wind it. I thought that was a bit harsh so I gave it a dead leg instead.
- I was at a cash point yesterday when a little old lady asked if I could check her balance. So I pushed her over.
- I start a new job in Seoul next week. I thought it was a good Korea move.
- I was driving this morning when I saw an RAC van parked up. The driver was sobbing uncontrollably and looked very miserable. I thought to myself, 'that guy's heading for a breakdown.'
- On holiday recently in Spain I saw a sign that said 'English speaking doctor.' I thought, 'What a good idea, why don't we have them in our country?'

Patent Brilliance

- A solar-powered submarine
- A Parachute that opens on impact
- Pedal wheel-chairs
- L-shaped mobile homes
- One-piece jig saw
- Inflatable dart-board
- Beer glasses with square bases so that they don't leave rings on the table
- Fireproof matches
- Solar-powered torch
- A book on how to read
- An index for a dictionary
- Ejection seats for helicopters
- Waterproof towels
- Waterproof teabags
- Electric windows for submarines

Politics Explained

A little boy asks his father, 'What is Politics?'

Dad says, 'Well son, let me try to explain it this way: I am the head of the family, so call me The Prime Minister. Your mother is the administrator of the money, so we call her the Government. We are here to take care of your needs, so we will call you the People. The nanny, we will consider her the Working Class. And your baby brother, we will call him the Future. Now think about that and see if it makes sense.'

So the little boy goes off to bed thinking about what Dad has said. Later that night, he hears his baby brother crying, so he gets up to check on him. He finds that the baby has severely soiled his nappy. So the little boy goes to his parent's room and finds his mother asleep. He creeps up the hall to look in the nanny's room. Through the keyhole and sees his father in bed with the nanny.

He gives up and goes back to bed.

The next morning, the little boy says to his father, 'Dad, I think I understand the concept of politics now. '

The father says, 'Good, son, tell me in your own words what you think politics is all about.'

The little boy replies, 'The Prime Minister is screwing the Working Class while the Government is sound asleep. The People are being ignored and the Future is in deep shit.'

Persistence

- Woody Allen - Academy Award-winning writer, producer and director - flunked motion picture production at New York University and the City College of New York. He also failed English at New York University.
- Leon Uris, author of the bestseller Exodus, failed high school English three times.
- When Lucille Ball began studying to be an actress in 1927, she was told by the head instructor of the John Murray Anderson Drama School, 'Try any other profession. Any other.'
- In 1959, a Universal Pictures executive dismissed Clint Eastwood and Burt Reynolds at the same meeting with the following statements. To Burt Reynolds: 'You have no talent.' To Clint Eastwood: 'You have a chip on your tooth, your Adam's apple sticks out too far and you talk too slow.' As you no doubt know, Burt Reynolds and Clint Eastwood went on to become big stars in the movie industry.
- In 1944, Emmeline Snively, director of the Blue Book Modeling Agency, told modeling hopeful Norma Jean Baker (Marilyn Monroe), 'You'd better learn secretarial work or else get married.'
- In 1962, four nervous young musicians played their first record audition for the executives of the Decca Recording Company. The executives were not impressed. While turning down this British rock group called the Beatles, one executive said, 'We don't like their sound. Groups of guitars are on the way out.'
- In 1954, Jimmy Denny, manager of the Grand Ole Opry, fired Elvis Presley after one performance. He told Presley, 'You ain't goin' nowhere son. You ought to go back to drivin' a truck.' Elvis Presley went on to become the most popular singer in America.
- When Alexander Graham Bell invented the telephone in 1876, it did not ring off the hook with calls from potential backers. After making a demonstration call, President Rutherford Hayes said, 'That's an amazing invention, but who would ever want to use one of them?'
- In the 1940s, a young inventor named Chester Carlson took his idea to 20 corporations, including some of the biggest in the country. They all turned him down. In 1947, after seven long years of

rejections, he finally got a tiny company in Rochester (the Haloid Company), New York, to purchase the rights to his electrostatic paper-copying process. Haloid became Xerox Corporation, and both it and Carlson became very rich.
- John Milton became blind at age 44. Sixteen years later he wrote the classic *Paradise Lost*.
- Franklin D. Roosevelt was paralyzed by polio at the age of 39, and yet he went on to become one of America's most beloved and influential leaders. He was elected president of the United States four times.
- When Pablo Casals reached 95, a young reporter threw him the following question. 'Mr. Casals, you are 95 and the greatest cellist that ever lived. Why do you still practice six hours a day?' Mr. Casals answered, 'Because I think I'm making progress.'
- After having his cancer-ridden leg amputated, young Canadian Terry Fox vowed to run on one leg from coast to coast the entire length of Canada to raise $1 million for cancer research. Forced to quit halfway when the cancer invaded his lungs, he and the foundation he started, had raised over $20 million for cancer research.
- Wilma Rudolph was the 20th of 22 children. She was born prematurely and her survival was doubtful. When she was 4 years old, she contracted double pneumonia and scarlet fever, which left her with a paralyzed left leg. At age 9, she removed the metal leg brace she had been dependent on and began to walk without it. By 13 she had developed a rhythmic walk, which doctors said was a miracle. That same year she decided to become a runner. She entered a race and came in last. For the next few years every race she entered, she came in last. Everyone told her to quit, but she kept on running. One day she actually won a race. And then another. From then on she won every race she entered. Eventually this little girl, who was told she would never walk again, went on to win three Olympic gold medals.
- Sarah Bernhardt, who is regarded by many as one of the greatest actresses who ever lived, had her leg amputated as a result of an injury when she was 70 years old, but she continued to act for the next eight years.
- Louis L'Amour, successful author of over 100 western novels with over 200 million copies in print, received 350 rejections before he

made his first sale. He later became the first American novelist to receive a special congressional gold medal in recognition of his distinguished career as an author and contributor to the nation through his historically based works.

One man …
Failed in business at age 21.
Was defeated in a legislative race at age 22.
Failed again in business at age 24.
Overcame the death of his sweetheart at age 26.
Had a nervous breakdown at age 27.
Lost a congressional race at age 34.
Lost a congressional race at age 36.
Lost a senatorial race at age 45.
Failed in an effort to become vice-president at age 47.
Lost a senatorial race at age 49.
Was elected president of the United States at age 52.

The man's name was Abraham Lincoln. Could he have become president if he had seen these events as failures? The whole world knows about this man's 'failures' but does it think any less of him for that? No, it admires him. Perhaps we should all try to make a few more mistakes and the world could be a better place.

Pertinent Facts

1. It takes 7 seconds for food to pass from mouth to stomach.
2. A human hair can hold 3kg.
3. The length of a penis is 3 times the length of the thumb.
4. The femur is as hard as concrete.
5. A woman's heart beats faster than a man's.
6. Women blink twice as often as men.
7. We use 300 muscles just to keep our balance when we stand.
8. A woman has read this entire post.
9. A man is still looking at his thumb.

Prayers For A New USA

By a 15-year-old school child in Arizona, USA – the new pledge of Allegiance, since the Lord's Prayer is not allowed to be said in most USA schools any more ...

Now I sit me down in school,
Where praying is against the rule,
For this great nation under God,
Finds mention of Him very odd.

If scripture now the class recites,
It violates the Bill of Rights.
And anytime my head I bow,
Becomes a Federal matter now.

Our hair can be purple, orange or green,
That's no offense; it's a freedom scene.
The law is specific, the law is precise.
Prayers spoken aloud are a serious vice.

For praying in a public hall,
Might offend someone with no faith at all.
In silence alone we must meditate,
God's name is prohibited by the state.

We're allowed to cuss and dress like freaks,
And pierce our noses, tongues and cheeks.
They've outlawed guns, but FIRST the Bible.
To quote the Good Book makes me liable.

We can elect a pregnant Senior Queen,
And the 'unwed daddy,' our Senior King.
It's 'inappropriate' to teach right from wrong,
We're taught that such 'judgments' do not belong.

Philip J Bradbury

We can get our condoms and birth controls,
Study witchcraft, vampires and totem poles.
But the Ten Commandments are not allowed,
No word of God must reach this crowd.

It's scary here I must confess,
When chaos reigns the school's a mess.
So, Lord, this silent plea I make:
Should I be shot, my soul please take!
Amen

Priest's Sermon Correction

A new priest at his first mass was so nervous he could hardly speak. After mass he asked the monsignor how he had done.

The monsignor replied, 'When I am worried about getting nervous on the pulpit, I put a glass of vodka next to the water glass. If I start to get nervous, I take a sip.'

Next Sunday he took the monsignor's advice. At the beginning of the sermon, he got nervous and took a drink. He proceeded to talk up a storm. Upon his return to his office after the mass, he found the following note on the door:

- Sip the vodka, don't gulp.
- There are 10 commandments, not 12.
- There are 12 disciples, not 10.
- Jesus was consecrated, not constipated.
- Jacob wagered his donkey, he did not bet his ass.
- We do not refer to Jesus Christ as the late J.C.
- The Father, Son, and Holy Ghost are not referred to as Daddy, Junior and the spook.
- David slew Goliath, he did not kick the shit out of him.
- When David was hit by a rock and was knocked off his donkey, don't say he was stoned off his ass.
- We do not refer to the cross as the 'Big T.'
- When Jesus broke the bread at the last supper he said, 'take this and eat it for it is my body.' He did not say 'Eat me …'
- The Virgin Mary is not called 'Mary with the Cherry'
- The recommended grace before a meal is not: Rub-A-Dub-Dub thanks for the grub, Yeah God.
- Next Sunday there will be a taffy pulling contest at St. Peter's, not a peter-pulling contest at St. Taffy's.

Puns

- Two antennas met on a roof, fell in love and got married. The ceremony wasn't much, but the reception was excellent.
- A set of jump leads walk into a bar. The bartender says, 'I'll serve you, but don't start anything.'
- Two peanuts walk into a bar, and one was a salted.
- A dyslexic man walks into a bra.
- A man walks into a bar with a slab of asphalt under his arm, and says: 'A beer please, and one for the road.'
- Two cannibals are eating a clown. One says to the other: 'Does this taste funny to you?'
- 'Doc, I can't stop singing 'The Green, Green Grass of Home.' 'That sounds like Tom Jones Syndrome.' 'Is it common?' 'Well, It's Not Unusual.'
- Two cows are standing next to each other in a field. Daisy says to Dolly, 'I was artificially inseminated this morning.' 'I don't believe you,' says Dolly. 'It's true; no bull!' exclaims Daisy.
- An invisible man marries an invisible woman. The kids were nothing to look at either.
- Deja Moo: The feeling that you've heard this bull before.
- I went to buy some camouflage trousers the other day, but I couldn't find any.
- A man woke up in a hospital after a serious accident. He shouted, 'Doctor, doctor, I can't feel my legs!'
  The doctor replied, 'I know you can't - I've cut off your arms!'
- I went to a seafood disco last week...and pulled a mussel.

- What do you call a fish with no eyes? A fsh..
- Two fish swim into a concrete wall. One turns to the other and says, 'Dam!'
- Two Eskimos sitting in a kayak were a bit cold, so they lit a fire in the craft. It sank, proving once again that you can't have your kayak and heat it too.
- A group of chess enthusiasts checked into a hotel, and were standing in the lobby discussing their recent tournament victories. After about an hour, the manager came out of the office, and asked them to disperse. 'But why,' they asked, as they moved off. 'Because,' he said, 'I can't stand chess-nuts boasting in an open foyer.'
- A woman has twins, and gives them up for adoption. One of them goes to a family in Egypt, and is named 'Ahmal.' The other goes to a family in Spain; they name him 'Juan.' Years later, Juan sends a picture of himself to his birth mother. Upon receiving the picture, she tells her husband that she wishes she also had a picture of Ahmal. Her husband responds, 'They're twins! If you've seen Juan, you've seen Ahmal.'
- Mahatma Gandhi, as you know, walked barefoot most of the time, which produced an impressive set of calluses on his feet. He also ate very little, which made him rather frail and with his odd diet, he suffered from bad breath. This made him ..... A super-calloused fragile mystic hexed by halitosis.
- And finally, there was the person who sent twenty different puns to his friends, with the hope that at least ten of the puns would make them laugh. No pun in ten did.

Punning From Ireland

Murphy says to Paddy, "What ya talkin into an envelope for?"
"I'm sending a voicemail ya fool!"

Paddy says "Mick, I'm thinking of buying a Labrador."
"Blow that," says Mick, "have you seen how many of their owners go blind?"

19 paddies go to the cinema and the ticket lady asks "Why so many of you?"
Mick replies, "The film said 18 or over."

I was explaining to my wife last night that when you die you get reincarnated but must come back as a different creature. She said she would like to come back as a cow.
I said "You're obviously not listening."

Two Muslims have crashed a speedboat into the Thames barrier in London. Police think it might be the start of Ram-a-dam.

Sat opposite an Indian lady on the train today. She shut her eyes and stopped breathing. I thought she was dead, until I saw the red spot on her forehead and realised she was just on standby.

The wife was counting all the 5ps and 10ps out on the kitchen table when she suddenly got very angry and started shouting and crying for no reason. I thought to myself, "She's going through the change."

When I was in the pub I heard a couple of plonkers saying that they wouldn't feel safe on an aircraft if they knew the pilot was a woman. What a pair of sexists. I mean, it's not as if she'd have to reverse the bloody thing!

Local police hunting the 'knitting needle nutter', who has stabbed six people in the rear in the last 48 hours, believe the attacker could be following some kind of pattern.

Bought some 'rocket salad' yesterday but it went off before I could eat it!

A teddy bear is working on a building site. He goes for a tea break and when he returns he notices his pick has been stolen. The bear is angry and reports the theft to the foreman. The foreman grins at the bear and says "Oh, I forgot to tell you, today's the day the teddy bears have their pick nicked."

Just got back from my mate's funeral. He died after being hit on the head with a tennis ball. It was a lovely service.

An Asian fellow has moved in next door. He has travelled the world, swum with sharks, wrestled bears and climbed the highest mountain. It came as no surprise to learn his name was Bindair Dundat.

An Irish priest is driving down the road and is pulled over for speeding. The garda smells alcohol on the priest's breath and then sees an empty wine bottle beside him.

   He asks the priest, "Sir, have you been drinking?"

   The priest responds, "No officer, just water,"

   The policeman asks, "Then why do I smell wine?"

   The priest looks at the bottle and says, "The Good Lord! He's done it again!"

Quotes

- America is the only country where a significant proportion of the population believes that professional wrestling is real but the moon landing was faked - David Letterman
- The average person thinks he isn't - Larry Lorenzoni
- Men are like linoleum floors. Lay 'em right and you can walk all over them for many years - Betsy Salkind
- When a man opens a car door for his wife, its either a new car or a new wife - Prince Phillip
- Lawyers believe a man is innocent until proven broke - Robin Hall
- Having more money doesn't make you happier. I have 50 million dollars but I'm just as happy as when I had 48 million - Arnold Schwarzenegger
- I was so poor that if I woke up on Christmas without an erection, I had nothing to play with - Frank McCourt
- When they circumcised you they threw away the wrong bit - David Lloyd Jones
- As I hurtled through space, one thought kept crossing my mind: every part of this rocket was supplied by the lowest bidder - John Glenn
- The first piece of luggage on the carousel never belongs to anyone - George Roberts
- The future isn't what it used to be - Yogi Berra

Red Skelton On Happy Marriage

1. Two times a week we go to a nice restaurant, have a little beverage, good food and companionship. She goes on Tuesdays, I go on Fridays.
2. We also sleep in separate beds. Hers is in California and mine is in Texas.
3. I take my wife everywhere but she keeps finding her way back.
4. I asked my wife where she wanted to go for our anniversary. "Somewhere I haven't been in a long time!" she said. So I suggested the kitchen.
5. We always hold hands. If I let go, she shops.
6. She has an electric blender, electric toaster and electric bread maker. She said "There are too many gadgets, and no place to sit down!" So I bought her an electric chair.
7. My wife told me the car wasn't running well because there was water in the carburettor. I asked where the car was. She told me, "In the lake."
8. She got a mud pack and looked great for two days. Then the mud fell off.
9. She ran after the garbage truck, yelling, "Am I too late for the garbage?" The driver said, "No, jump in!"
10. Remember: Marriage is the number one cause of divorce.
11. I married Miss Right. I just didn't know her first name was 'Always'.
12. I haven't spoken to my wife in 18 months. I don't like to interrupt her.
13. The last fight was my fault though. My wife asked, "What's on the TV?" I said, "Dust!"

Religious Questions

Laura Schlessinger is a US radio personality who dispenses advice to people who call in to her radio show. Recently, she said that, as an observant Orthodox Jew, she regards homosexuality as an abomination according to Leviticus 18:22 which cannot be condoned in any circumstance. The following is an open letter to Dr. Laura penned by a US resident, which was posted on the Internet.

Dear Dr. Laura:

Thank you for doing so much to educate people regarding God's Law. I have learned a great deal from your show, and I try to share that knowledge with as many people as I can. When someone tries to defend the homosexual lifestyle, for example, I simply remind them that Leviticus 18:22 clearly states it to be an abomination. End of debate. I do need some advice from you, however, regarding some of the specific laws and how to follow them.

When I burn a bull on the altar as a sacrifice, I know it creates a pleasing odour for the Lord (Lev. 1:9). The problem is my neighbours. They claim the odour is not pleasing to them. Should I smite them?

I would like to sell my daughter into slavery, as sanctioned in Exodus 21:7. In this day and age, what do you think would be a fair price for her?

I know that I am allowed no contact with a woman while she is in her period of menstrual uncleanliness (Lev. 15:19-24). The problem is, how do I tell? I have tried asking, but most women take offence.

Lev. 25:44 states that I may indeed possess slaves, both male and female, provided they are purchased from neighbouring nations. A friend of mine claims that this applies to Mexicans, but not Canadians. Can you clarify? Why can't I own Canadians?

I have a neighbour who insists on working on the Sabbath. Exodus 35:2 clearly states he should be put to death. Am I morally obligated to kill him myself?

A friend of mine feels that even though eating shellfish is an abomination (Lev. 11:10), it is a lesser abomination than homosexuality. I don't agree. Can you settle this?

Lev. 21:20 states that I may not approach the altar of God if I have a defect in my sight. I have to admit that I wear reading glasses. Does my vision have to be 20/20, or is there some wiggle room here?

Most of my male friends get their hair trimmed, including the hair around their temples, even though this is expressly forbidden by Lev. 19:27. How should they die?

I know from Lev. 11:6-8 that touching the skin of a dead pig makes me unclean, but may I still play football if I wear gloves?

My uncle has a farm. He violates Lev. 19:19 by planting two different crops in the same field, as does his wife by wearing garments made of two different kinds of thread (cotton/polyester blend). He also tends to curse and blaspheme a lot. Is it really necessary that we go to all the trouble of getting the whole town together to stone them? (Lev.24: 10-16) Couldn't we just burn them to death at a private family affair like we do with people who sleep with their in-laws? (Lev. 20:14)

School Exam Answers

Q: Name the four seasons.
A: Salt, pepper, mustard and vinegar.

Q: Explain one of the processes by which water can be made safe to drink.
A: Flirtation makes water safe to drink because it removes large pollutants like grit, sand, dead sheep and canoeists.

Q: How is dew formed?
A: The sun shines down on the leaves and makes them perspire.

Q: What is a planet?
A: A body of earth surrounded by sky.

Q: What causes the tides in the oceans?
A: The tides are a fight between the Earth and the Moon. All water tends to flow towards the moon because there is no water on the moon and nature abhors a vacuum. I forget where the sun joins in this fight.

Q: What guarantees may a mortgage company insist on?
A: If you are buying a house they will insist you are well endowed.

Q: What happens to your body as you age?
A: When you get old, so do your bowels and you get intercontinental.

Q: What happens to a boy when he reached puberty?
A: He says goodbye to his boyhood and looks forward to his adultery.

Q: Name a major disease associated with cigarettes.
A: Premature death.

Q: What is artificial insemination?
A: When the farmer does it to the bull instead of the cow.

Q: Give an example of movement in plants and an animal that cannot move.
A: Tryphids and a dead cat.

Historical explanations:
In midevil times most people were alliterate. The greatest writer of the futile ages was Chaucer who wrote many poems and verses and also wrote literature.

Gravity was invented by Isaac Walton. It is chiefly noticeable in the autumn what the apples are falling off the trees.

Beethoven wrote music even though he was deaf. He was so deaf he wrote loud music. He took long walks in the forest even when everyone was calling for him. Beethoven expired in 1827 and later died for this.

Queen Victoria was the longest queen. She sat on the thorn for 63 years. She was a moral woman who practised virtue. Her death was the final event that ended her reign.

Macbeth is a cowardly custard. His wife was sex starved and he gets his come-uppance because, as my mum always sez, wot goes around comes around.

Lady Macbeth sez to Macbeth, 'sort your head out'.

When Macbeth hears of Lady Macbeth's death he goes full-on soliloquy mode.

Lady Macbeth had a desire to have Macbeth on the throne and asked him to show her his manhood.

The witches and the dagger weren't there, Macbeth had been smoking up and imagined them all.

When asked how the balcony scene ended in Romeo and Juliet one student offered, 'they jumped in the swimming pool. He had been watching the modern film version.

Macbeth is like a snail shell without a snail when Lady Macbeth dies.

Scientific Explanation

A scientist being interviewed after finding a man who could create rain:

'I'm afraid we can't comment on the name Rain God at this present time, and we are calling him an example of Spontaneous Para-Causal Meteorological Phenomenon.'

'Can you tell us what that means?'

'I'm not altogether sure. Let's be straight here. If we find something we can't understand we like to call it something you can't understand, or even pronounce. I mean if we just let you go around calling him a Rain God, then that suggests that you know something we don't, and I'm afraid we couldn't have that.

'No, first we have to call it something which says it's ours, not yours, then we set about finding some way of proving it's not what you said it is, but something we say it is.

'And if it turns out you're right, you'll still be wrong because we will simply call him a … er, Supernormal … - not paranormal or supernatural because you think you know what those mean now, no, a Supernormal Incremental Precipitation Inducer. We'll probably want to shove a Quasi in there somewhere to protect ourselves. Rain God! Huh, never heard such nonsense in my life.'

So Long, and Thanks For All the Fish by Douglas Adams.

Senior's Bank Letter

A 98 year old woman in the UK wrote this to her bank. The bank manager thought it amusing enough to have it published in the Times.

Dear Sir,

I am writing to thank you for bouncing my cheque with which I endeavoured to pay my plumber last month. By my calculations, three nanoseconds must have elapsed between his presenting the cheque and the arrival in my account of the funds needed to honour it. I refer, of course, to the automatic monthly deposit of my Pension, an arrangement, which, I admit, has been in place for only thirty eight years. You are to be commended for seizing that brief window of opportunity, and also for debiting my account £30 by way of penalty for the inconvenience caused to your bank.

My thankfulness springs from the manner in which this incident has caused me to rethink my errant financial ways. I noticed that whereas I personally attend to your telephone calls and letters, when I try to contact you, I am confronted by the impersonal, overcharging, pre-recorded, faceless entity which your bank has become. From now on, I, like you, choose only to deal with a flesh-and- blood person.

My mortgage and loan payments will therefore and hereafter no longer be automatic, but will arrive at your bank by cheque, addressed personally and confidentially to an employee at your bank whom you must nominate. Be aware that it is an offence under the Postal Act for any other person to open such an envelope. Please find attached an Application Contact Status which I require your chosen employee to complete. I am sorry it runs to eight pages, but in order that I know as much about him or her as your bank knows about me, there is no alternative. Please note that all copies of his or her medical history must be countersigned by a Solicitor, and the mandatory details of his/her financial situation (income, debts, assets and liabilities) must be accompanied by documented proof.

In due course, I will issue your employee with PIN number which he/she must quote in dealings with me. I regret that it cannot be shorter than 28 digits but, again, I have modelled it on the number of button presses required of me to access my account balance on your phone bank service. As they say, imitation is the sincerest form of flattery.

Let me level the playing field even further. When you call me, press buttons as follows:

1. To make an appointment to see me.
2. To query a missing payment.
3. To transfer the call to my living room in case I am there.
4. To transfer the call to my bedroom in case I am sleeping.
5. To transfer the call to my toilet in case I am attending to nature.
6. To transfer the call to my mobile phone if I am not at home.
7. To leave a message on my computer (a password to access my computer is required. A password will be communicated to you at a later date to the Authorized Contact.)
8. To return to the main menu and to listen to options 1 through to 8.
9. To make a general complaint or inquiry, the contact will then be put on hold, pending the attention of my automated answering service. While this may, on occasion, involve a lengthy wait, uplifting music will play for the duration of the call.

Regrettably, but again following your example, I must also levy an establishment fee to cover the setting up of this new arrangement.

May I wish you a happy, if ever so slightly less prosperous New Year.

Your Humble Client

Senior Health Care Plan

So you're a senior citizen and your government tells you it has no nursing homes available to you. What do you do?

Our plan gives anyone 65 and over a revolver and four bullets. You can shoot 2 MPs and 2 Ministers – not necessarily dead.

Of course, this means that you'll be sent to prison where you'll three meals a day, a roof over your head, central heating and all the health care you need! Need new teeth – no problem. New glasses – no problem. New hip, knee, kidney, lungs, heart? All covered. And your kids can come and visit as often as they do now.

And who will pay for this? The same government that told you it couldn't afford for you to go into a nursing home.

And, because you are a prisoner, you won't have to pay income taxes either.

Is this country great or what!

Sex Quotes

- "I believe that sex is one of the most beautiful, natural, wholesome things that money can buy." Tom Clancy
- "Women might be able to fake orgasms. But men can fake whole relationships." Sharon Stone
- "You know "that look" women get when they want sex? Me neither." Steve Martin
- "There are a number of mechanical devices which increase sexual arousal, particularly in women. Chief among these is the Mercedes-Benz 500SL." Lynn Lavner
- "According to a new survey, women say they feel more comfortable undressing in front of men than they do undressing in front of other women. They say that women are too judgmental, where, of course, men are just grateful." Robert De Niro
- "Sex at age 90 is like trying to shoot pool with a rope." Camille Paglia
- "Sex is one of the nine reasons for reincarnation. The other eight are unimportant." George Burns
- "Bisexuality immediately doubles your chances for a date on Saturday night." Rodney Dangerfield
- "My girlfriend always laughs during sex ~ no matter what she's reading." Steve Jobs (Founder, Apple Computers)
- "Hockey is a sport for white men. Basketball is a sport for black men. Golf is a sport for white men dressed like black pimps." Tiger Woods

- "My mother never saw the irony in calling me a son-of-a-bitch." Jack Nicholson
- "Clinton lied. A man might forget where he parks or where he lives, but he never forgets oral sex, no matter how bad it is." Barbara Bush (Former US First Lady, and you didn't think Barbara had a sense of humor!)
- "Ah, yes, Divorce, from the Latin word meaning to rip out a man's genitals through his wallet." Robin Williams
- "Women need a reason to have sex. Men just need a place." Billy Crystal
- "There's a new medical crisis. Doctors are reporting that many men are having allergic reactions to latex condoms. They say they cause severe swelling. So what's the problem?" Dustin Hoffman
- "Instead of getting married again, I'm going to find a woman I don't like and just give her a house." Rod Stewart
- "See, the problem is that God gives men a brain and a penis, and only enough blood to run one at a time." Robin Williams

Smart Alec Answers

It was mealtime during a flight on American Airlines. "Would you like dinner?" the flight attendant asked John, seated in front.
"What are my choices?" John asked.
"Yes or no," she replied.

A flight attendant was stationed at the departure gate to check tickets. As a man approached, she extended her hand for the ticket and he opened his trench coat and flashed her.
Without missing a beat, she said, "Sir, I need to see your ticket not your stub."

A lady was picking through the frozen turkeys at the grocery store but she couldn't find one big enough for her family. She asked a stock boy, "Do these turkeys get any bigger?"
The stock boy replied, "No ma'am, they're dead."

The cop got out of his car and the kid who was stopped for speeding rolled down his window.
"I've been waiting for you all day," the cop said.
The kid replied, "Yeah, well I got here as fast as I could."

A truck driver was driving along on the freeway. A sign comes up that reads, "Low Bridge Ahead". Before he knows it, the bridge is right ahead of him and he gets stuck under the bridge. Cars are backed up for miles. Finally, a police car comes up. The cop gets out of his car and walks to the truck driver, puts his hands on his hips and says, "Got stuck, huh?"

The truck driver says, "No, I was delivering this bridge and ran out of gas."

A college teacher reminds her class of tomorrow's final exam. "Now class, I won't tolerate any excuses or you not being here tomorrow. I might consider a nuclear attack or a serious personal injury, illness, or a death in your immediate family, but that's it, no other excuses whatsoever!"

A smart-ass guy in the back of the room raised his hand and asked, "What would you say if tomorrow I said I was suffering from complete and utter sexual exhaustion?" The entire class is reduced to laughter and snickering.

When silence is restored, the teacher smiles knowingly at the student, shakes her head and sweetly says, "Well, I guess you'd have to write the exam with your other hand."

`Sometimes ...`

Sometimes when you cry ...
No one sees your tears.

Sometimes when you are in pain ...
No one sees your hurt.

Sometimes when you are worried ...
No one sees your stress.

Sometimes when you are happy ...
No one sees your smile.

But FART!! just ONE time ...

Sydney Olympic Questions

Questions to the Sydney Olympics information line:
- Does it ever get windy in Australia? I have never seen it rain on TV, so how do the plants grow? (UK)
- Will I be able to see kangaroos in the street? (USA) (Depends on how much beer you've consumed...)
- Which direction should I drive - Perth to Darwin or Darwin to Perth - to avoid driving with the sun in my eyes? (Germany) (Excellent question, considering that the Olympics are being held in Sydney)
- I want to walk from Perth to Sydney - can I follow the railroad tracks? (Sweden) (Sure, it's only seven thousand miles, so you'll need to have started about a year and a half ago to get there in time for this October...)
- Is it safe to run around in the bushes in Australia? (Sweden) (And accomplish what?)
- It is imperative that I find the names and addresses of places to contact for a stuffed porpoise. (Italy) (Not touching this one...)
- My client wants to take a steel pooper-scooper into Australia. Will you let her in? (South Africa) (Why? We do have toilet paper here...)
- Are there any ATMs in Australia? Can you send me a list of them in Brisbane, Cairns, Townsville and Hervey Bay? (UK)
- Where can I learn underwater welding in Australia? (Portugal)
- Do the camels in Australia have one hump or two? (UK)
- Can I bring cutlery into Australia? (UK) (Why bother? Use your fingers like the rest of us...)

- Do you have perfume in Australia? (France) (No. Everybody stinks.)
- Do tents exist in Australia? (Germany)
- Can I wear high heels in Australia? (UK) (This HAS to have been asked by a blonde...)
- Can you tell me the regions in Tasmania where the female population is smaller than the male population? (Italy) (Yes. Gay nightclubs.)
- Do you celebrate Christmas in Australia? (France) (Yes, at Christmas.)
- Can I drive to the Great Barrier Reef? (Germany) (Sure, if your vehicle is amphibious.)
- Are there killer bees in Australia? (Germany) (Not yet, but we'll see what we can do when you get here.)
- Can you give me some information about hippo racing in Australia? (USA) (What's this guy smoking?)
- Are there supermarkets in Sydney and is milk available all year round? (Germany) (Another blonde?)
- Please send a list of all doctors in Australia who can dispense rattlesnake serum. (USA) (There are no rattlesnakes in Australia)
- Which direction is North in Australia? (USA) (probably from the CIA)
- Can you send me the Vienna Boys' Choir schedule? (USA) (Americans have long had considerable trouble distinguishing between Austria and Australia … and a few other things me thinks)
- I have a question about a famous animal in Australia, but I forget its name. It's a kind of bear and lives in trees. (USA)
- I have developed a new product that is the fountain of youth. Can you tell me where I can sell it in Australia? (USA)
- Are there places in Australia where you can make love outdoors? (Italy) (Yes. Outdoors.)
- I was in Australia in 1969 on R+R, and I want to contact the girl I dated while I was staying in Kings Cross. Can you help? (USA) (This guy's got it coming!)
- Will I be able to speak English most places I go? (USA) (Not if you can't now.)

Teacher Arrested

NEW YORK - A public school teacher was arrested today at John F. Kennedy International Airport as he attempted to board a flight while in possession of a ruler, a protractor, a set square, a slide rule and a calculator.

At a morning press conference, Attorney General Alberto Gonzales said he believes the man is a member of the notorious Al-gebra movement. He did not identify the man, who has been charged by the FBI with carrying weapons of math instruction. "Al-gebra is a problem for us," Gonzales said. "They desire solutions by means and extremes, and sometimes go off on tangents in search of absolute values. They use secret code names like 'x' and 'y' and refer to themselves as 'unknowns', but we have determined they belong to a common denominator of the axis of medieval with coordinates in every country.

As the Greek philanderer Isosceles used to say, 'There are 3 sides to every triangle'."

When asked to comment on the arrest, President Bush said, "If God had wanted us to have better weapons of math instruction, he would have given us more fingers and toes." White House aides told reporters they could not recall a more intelligent or profound statement by the president.

Terrorist Alerts Around The World

The English are feeling the pinch in relation to recent terrorist threats and have raised their security level from "Miffed" to "Peeved." Soon, though, security levels may be raised yet again to "Irritated" or even "A Bit Cross." The English have not been "A Bit Cross" since the blitz in 1940 when tea supplies all but ran out. Terrorists have been re-categorized from "Tiresome" to a "Bloody Nuisance." The last time the British issued a "Bloody Nuisance" warning level was during the great fire of 1666.

The Scots raised their threat level from "Pissed Off" to "Let's get the Bastards". They don't have any other levels. This is the reason they have been used on the front line in the British army for the last 300 years.

The French government announced yesterday that it has raised its terror alert level from "Run" to "Hide". The only two higher levels in France are "Collaborate" and "Surrender." The rise was precipitated by a recent fire that destroyed France's white flag factory, effectively paralysing the country's military capability. It's not only the French who are on a heightened level of alert. Italy has increased the alert level from "Shout loudly and excitedly" to "Elaborate Military Posturing." Two more levels remain: "Ineffective Combat Operations" and "Change Sides."

The Germans also increased their alert state from "Disdainful Arrogance" to "Dress in Uniform and Sing Marching Songs." They also have two higher levels: "Invade a Neighbour" and "Lose".

Belgians, on the other hand, are all on holiday as usual, and the only threat they are worried about is NATO pulling out of Brussels.

The Spanish are all excited to see their new submarines ready to deploy. These beautifully designed subs have glass bottoms so the new Spanish navy can get a really good look at the old Spanish navy.

Americans, meanwhile, are, as usual, carrying out pre-emptive strikes, on all of their allies, just in case.

New Zealand has also raised its security levels - from "baaa" to "BAAAA!" Due to continuing defence cutbacks (the air-force being a squadron of spotty teenagers flying paper aeroplanes and the navy some toy boats in the Prime Minister's bath), New Zealand only has one more level of escalation, which is "Shit, I hope Australia will come and rescue us".

Australia, meanwhile, has raised its security level from "No worries" to "She'll be right, mate". Three more escalation levels remain: "Crikey!", "I think we'll need to cancel the barbie this weekend" and "The barbie is cancelled". So far no situation has ever warranted use of the final escalation level.

Toilet Rules

STAFF NOTICE
With immediate effect, a toilet policy will be established to provide for a more consistent method of accounting for staff, ensuring effective time management and equal treatment for all.

On the first day of every month all staff will be issued 20 toilet trip credits. These may be accumulated. The doors to all toilets will be equipped with computer-linked voice recognition devices. Staff must immediately provide management with two voice prints, one normal and one under stress.

Once the employee toilet bank reaches zero, the doors to the toilet will not unlock for the employee's voice until the first of the month.

In addition, all cubicles will be equipped with timed paper roll retractors. If the toilet is occupied for more than three minutes, an alarm will sound. Thirty seconds later, the roll of toilet paper will retract into the dispenser, the toilet will flush and the door will open automatically.

If the toilet remains occupied, your photograph will be taken by a security camera and will appear on the Toilet Offenders Board. Anyone appearing three times will forfeit three months trip credits.

Anyone caught smiling when the photograph is taken will undergo counselling by a clinical psychologist.

Be advised that accident compensation insurance does not cover injuries while trying to stop the toilet paper retracting into the dispenser.

Travellers' Instructions

- In a Tokyo Hotel: Is forbitten to steal hotel towels please. If you are not person to do such thing is please not to read notis.
- In a Vienna hotel: In case of fire, do your utmost to alarm the hotel porter.
- From a Japanese information booklet about using a hotel air conditioner: Cooles and Heates: If you want just condition of warm in your room, please control yourself.
- In another Japanese hotel room: Please to bathe inside the tub.
- In a Bucharest hotel lobby: The lift is being fixed for the next day. During that time we regret that you will be unbearable.
- In a Belgrade hotel elevator: To move the cabin, push button for wishing floor. If the cabin should enter more persons, each one should press a number of wishing floor. Driving is then going alphabetically by national order.
- In a Leipzig elevator: Do not enter the lift backwards, and only when lit up.
- Two signs from a Majorcan shop entrance:
  English well talking.
  Here speeching American.
- In a Yugoslavian hotel: The flattening of underwear with pleasure is the job of the chambermaid.
- In the lobby of a Moscow hotel across from a Russian Orthodox monastery: You are welcome to visit the cemetery where famous Russian and Soviet composers, artists, and writers are buried daily except Thursday.
- In an Austrian hotel catering to skiers: Not to perambulate the corridors in the hours of repose in the boots of ascension.
- On the menu of a Swiss restaurant: Our wines leave you nothing to hope for.
- On the menu of a Polish hotel: Salad a firm's own make; limpid red beet soup with cheesy dumplings in the form of a finger; roasted duck let loose; beef rashers beaten up in the country people's fashion.
- In a Hong Kong supermarket: For your convenience, we recommend courageous, efficient self-service.

- Outside a Hong Kong tailor shop: Ladies may have a fit upstairs.
- Outside a Paris dress shop: Dresses for street walking.
- In a Bangkok dry cleaner's: Drop your trousers here for best results.
- Similarly, from the Soviet Weekly: There will be a Moscow Exhibition of Arts by 15,000 Soviet Republic painters and sculptors. These were executed over the past two years.
- In an East African newspaper: A new swimming pool is rapidly taking shape since the contractors have thrown in the bulk of their workers.
- In a Japanese hotel: You are invited to take advantage of the chambermaid.
- A sign posted in Germany's Black Forest: It is strictly forbidden on our black forest camping site that people of different sex, for instance, men and women, live together in one tent unless they are married with each other for that purpose.
- In a Zurich hotel: Because of the impropriety of entertaining guests of the opposite sex in the bedroom, it is suggested that the lobby be used for this purpose.
- In an advertisement by a Hong Kong dentist: Teeth extracted by the latest Methodists.
- A translated sentence from a Russian chess book: A lot of water has been passed under the bridge since this variation has been played.
- In a Rome laundry: Ladies, leave your clothes here and spend the afternoon having a good time.
- In a Czechoslovakian tourist agency: Take one of our horse-driven city tours – we guarantee no miscarriages.
- Advertisement for donkey rides in Thailand: Would you like to ride on your own ass?
- On the faucet in a Finnish washroom: To stop the drip, turn cock to right.
- In the window of a Swedish furrier: Fur coats made for ladies from their own skin.
- On the box of a clockwork toy made in Hong Kong: Guaranteed to work throughout its useful life.
- Detour sign in Kyushi, Japan: Stop: Drive Sideways.
- In a Swiss mountain inn: Special today – no ice cream.
- In a Bangkok temple: It is forbidden to enter a woman even a foreigner if dressed as a man.

- In a Tokyo bar: Special cocktails for the ladies with nuts.
- In a Copenhagen airline ticket office: We take your bags and send them in all directions.
- On the door of a Moscow hotel room: If this is your first visit to the USSR, you are welcome to it.
- In a Norwegian cocktail lounge: Ladies are requested not to have children in the bar.
- At a Budapest zoo: Please do not feed the animals. If you have any suitable food, give it to the guard on duty.
- In the office of a Roman doctor: Specialist in women and other diseases.
- In an Acapulco hotel: The manager has personally passed all the water served here.
- In a Tokyo shop: Our nylons cost more than common, but you'll find they are best in the long run.
- In a Paris hotel elevator: Please leave your values at the front desk.
- From a brochure of a car rental firm in Tokyo: When passenger of foot heave in sight, tootle the horn. Trumpet him melodiously at first, but if he still obstacles your passage then tootle him with vigor.

A clerk at a Philadelphia airline counter picked up the telephone and heard the caller ask, "How long does it take to go from Philadelphia to Phoenix ?"

She was busy with another customer just then and intended to put the caller on hold. "Just a minute," she replied.

As she was about to press the hold button, the caller said, "Thank you," and hung up.

Unexpected Angels

As she stood in front of her 5th grade class on the very first day of school, she told the children an untruth. Like most teachers, she looked at her students and said that she loved them all the same. However, that was impossible because, there in the front row, slumped in his seat, was a little boy named Teddy Stoddard. Mrs Thompson had watched Teddy the year before and noticed that he did not play well with the other children, that his clothes were messy and that he constantly needed a bath. In addition, Teddy could be unpleasant. It got to the point where Mrs Thompson would actually take delight in marking his papers with a broad red pen, making bold X's and then putting a big "F" at the top of his papers.

At the school where Mrs Thompson taught, she was required to review each child's past records and she put Teddy's off until last. However, when she reviewed his file, she was in for a surprise. Teddy's first grade teacher wrote, "Teddy is a bright child with a ready laugh. He does his work neatly and has good manners ... he is a joy to be around." His second grade teacher wrote, "Teddy is an excellent student, well liked by his classmates but he is troubled because his mother has a terminal illness and life at home must be a struggle." His third grade teacher wrote, "His mother's death has been hard on him. He tries to do his best, but his father doesn't show much interest and his home life will soon affect him if some steps aren't taken." Teddy's fourth grade teacher wrote, "Teddy is withdrawn and doesn't show much interest in school. He doesn't have many friends and he sometimes sleeps in class."

By now, Mrs Thompson realized the problem and she was ashamed of herself. She felt even worse when her students brought her Christmas presents, wrapped in beautiful ribbons and bright paper, except for Teddy's. His present was clumsily wrapped in the heavy, brown paper that he got from a grocery bag. Mrs Thompson took pains to open it in the middle of the other presents. Some of the children started to laugh when she found a rhinestone bracelet with some of the stones missing, and a bottle that was one-quarter full of perfume. But she stifled the children's laughter when she exclaimed how pretty the bracelet was, putting it on, and dabbing some of the perfume on her wrist.

Teddy Stoddard stayed after school that day just long enough to say, "Mrs Thompson, today you smelled just like my Mom used to."

After the children left, she cried for at least an hour. On that very day, she quit teaching reading, writing and arithmetic. Instead, she began to teach children. Mrs Thompson paid particular attention to Teddy. As she worked with him, his mind seemed to come alive. The more she encouraged him, the faster he responded. By the end of the year, Teddy had become one of the smartest children in the class and, despite her lie that she would love all the children the same, Teddy became one of her "teacher's pets."

A year later, she found a note under her door, from Teddy, telling her that she was still the best teacher he ever had in his whole life. Six years went by before she got another note from Teddy. He then wrote that he had finished high school, third in his class, and she was still the best teacher he ever had in life. Four years after that, she got another letter, saying that while things had been tough at times, he'd stayed in school, had stuck with it, and would soon graduate from college with the highest of honours. He assured Mrs Thompson that she was still the best and favourite teacher he had ever had in his whole life. Then four more years passed and yet another letter came. This time he explained that after he got his bachelor's degree, he decided to go a little further. The letter explained that she was still the best and favourite teacher he ever had But now his name was a little longer ... The letter was signed, Theodore F. Stoddard, MD.

There was yet another letter that spring. Teddy said he had met this girl and was going to be married. He explained that his father had died a couple of years ago and he was wondering if Mrs Thompson might agree to sit at the wedding in the place that was usually reserved for the mother of the groom. Of course, Mrs Thompson did. And guess what? She wore that bracelet, the one with several rhinestones missing. Moreover, she made sure she was wearing the perfume that Teddy remembered his mother wearing on their last Christmas together.

They hugged each other, and Dr Stoddard whispered in Mrs Thompson's ear, "Thank you Mrs Thompson for believing in me. Thank you so much for making me feel important and showing me that I could make a difference."

Mrs Thompson, with tears in her eyes, whispered back, "Teddy, you have it all wrong. You were the one who taught me that I could make a difference. I didn't know how to teach until I met you!"

Teddy Stoddard is the doctor at Iowa Methodist in Des Moines that has the Stoddard Cancer Wing.

Universal Wisdom

- My husband and I divorced over religious differences. He thought he was God and I didn't!
- I don't suffer from insanity. I enjoy every minute of it.
- I work hard because millions on welfare depend on me!
- Some people are alive only because it's illegal to kill them.
- I used to have a handle on life, but it broke.
- Don't take life too seriously; you won't get out alive.
- You're just jealous because the voices only talk to me.
- Beauty is in the eye of the beer holder.
- Earth is the insane asylum for the universe.
- Quoting one is plagiarism; quoting many is research.
- I'm not a complete idiot; some parts are missing.
- Out of my mind. Back in five minutes.
- NyQuil - The stuffy, sneezy, coughing, why-oh-why-is-the-room spinning medicine.
- The trouble with life is there's no background music.
- God must love stupid people; he made so many.
- The gene pool could use a little chlorine.
- It IS as bad as you think and they ARE out to get you.
- I took an IQ test and the results were negative.
- Consciousness: that annoying time between naps.
- Ever stop to think, and forget to start again?
- To err is human, to really foul things up requires a computer.
- Wrinkled Was Not One of the Things I Wanted to Be When I Grew Up.
- Save the whales. Collect the whole set.
- A day without sunshine is like, night.
- On the other hand, you have different fingers.
- I just got lost in thought. It was unfamiliar territory.
- 42.7 percent of all statistics are made up on the spot.
- Ninety-nine percent of lawyers give the rest a bad name.
- I feel like I'm diagonally parked in a parallel universe.
- Honk if you love peace and quiet.

- Remember, half the people you know are below average.
- He who laughs last, thinks slowest.
- Depression is merely anger without enthusiasm.
- The early bird may get the worm, but the second mouse gets the cheese.
- I drive way too fast to worry about cholesterol.
- Support bacteria. They're the only culture some people have.
- Monday is an awful way to spend one-seventh of your life.
- A clear conscience is usually the sign of a bad memory.
- Change is inevitable, except from vending machines.
- Get a new car for your spouse. It'll be a great trade!
- Plan to be spontaneous ... tomorrow.
- Always try to be modest, and be proud of it!
- If you think nobody cares, try missing a couple of payments.
- How many of you believe in telekinesis? Raise my hand...
- OK, so what's the speed of dark?
- How do you tell when you're out of invisible ink?
- If everything seems to be going well, you have obviously overlooked something.
- When everything is coming your way, you're in the wrong lane.
- Hard work pays off in the future. Laziness pays off now.
- Everyone has a photographic memory; some just don't have film.
- If Barbie is so popular, why do you have to buy her friends?
- Eagles may soar, but weasels don't get sucked into jet engines.
- What happens if you get scared half to death twice?
- I used to have an open mind but my brains kept falling out.
- I couldn't repair your brakes, so I made your horn louder.
- Why do psychics have to ask you for your name
- Inside every older person is a younger person wondering 'WHAT THE HECK HAPPENED?!!!'

Unusual Body Finds

Inner Skeleton
A 63 yr. old widow was admitted to the hospital in Recife, Brazil, suffering abdominal pains. X-rays showed that she was carrying a 20 inch long skeleton of a foetus which she conceived decades earlier. It had become lodged outside the womb and was never expelled from her body.

Female sofa
A 500 lb. woman from Illinois was examined in a hospital. During the examination, an asthma inhaler fell from under her armpit, a dime was found under one of her breasts and a remote control was found lodged between the folds of her vulva.

Prickly pair
In Michigan, a man came into the ER with lacerations to his penis. He complained that his wife had a rat in her privates and it bit him during sex. After an examination of his wife, it was revealed that she had a surgical needle left inside her after a recent hysterectomy.

Ping pong anyone?
A twenty-year-old man came into the ER with a stony mass in his rectum. He said that he and his boyfriend were fooling around with concrete mix, then his boyfriend had the idea of pouring the mix into his anus using a funnel. The concrete then hardened, causing constipation and pain. Under general anaesthesia, a perfect concrete cast of the man's rectum was removed, along with a ping pong ball.

Blind drunk
A drunk staggered into a Pennsylvania ER complaining of severe pain while trying to remove his contact lenses. He said that they would come out halfway, but they always popped back in. A nurse tried to help using a suction pump, but without success. Finally, a doctor examined him and discovered the man did not have his contact lenses in at all. He had been trying to rip out the membrane of his cornea.

Ouch and double ouch!

A couple hobbled into a Washington (state) emergency room covered in bloody restaurant towels. The man had his around his waist and the woman had hers around her head. They eventually explained to doctors that they had gone out that evening for a romantic dinner. Overcome with passion, the woman crept under the table to administer oral sex to the man. While in the act she had an epileptic seizure, which caused her to clamp down on the man's penis and wrench it from side to side. In agony and desperation, the man grabbed a fork and stabbed her in the head until she let go.

Woman's Wisdom

- If you love something, set it free. If it comes back, it will always be yours. If it doesn't come back, it was never yours to begin with. But, if it just sits in your living room, messes up your stuff, eats your food, uses your telephone, takes your money, and doesn't appear to realize that you had set it free, you either married it or gave birth to it.
- A friend of mine confused her valium with her birth control pills. She has 14 kids but she doesn't really care.
- My mind not only wanders, it sometime leaves completely.
- I gave up jogging for my health when my thighs kept rubbing together and setting my pantyhose on fire.
- Skinny people irritate me! Especially when they say things like, 'You know, sometimes I just forget to eat.' Now I've forgotten` my address, my mother's maiden name, and my keys. But I've never forgotten to eat. You have to be a special kind of stupid to forget to eat.
- I read that the typical symptoms of stress are eating too much, impulse buying and driving too fast. Are they kidding? That's my idea of a perfect day.
- If men can run the world, why can't they stop wearing neckties? How intelligent is it to start the day by tying a noose around your neck?

Word Meanings

The Washington Post's Mensa Invitational once again invited readers to take any word from the dictionary, alter it by adding, subtracting, or changing one letter, and supply a new definition.

Here are the winners:
- Cashtration (n.): The act of buying a house, which renders the subject financially impotent for an indefinite period of time.
- Ignoranus: A person who's both stupid and an asshole.
- Intaxicaton: Euphoria at getting a tax refund, which lasts until you realize it was your money to start with.
- Reintarnation: Coming back to life as a hillbilly.
- Bozone (n.): The substance surrounding stupid people that stops bright ideas from penetrating The bozone layer, unfortunately, shows little sign of breaking down in the near future.
- Foreploy: Any misrepresentation about yourself for the purpose of getting laid.
- Giraffiti: Vandalism spray-painted very, very high
- Sarchasm: The gulf between the author of sarcastic wit and the person who doesn't get it.
- Inoculatte: To take coffee intravenously when you are running late.
- Osteopornosis: A degenerate disease.
- Karmageddon: It's like, when everybody is sending off all these really bad vibes, right? And then, like, the Earth explodes and it's like, a serious bummer.
- Decafalon (n.): The grueling event of getting through the day consuming only things that are good for you.
- Glibido: All talk and no action.
- Dopeler Effect: The tendency of stupid ideas to seem smarter when they come at you rapidly.
- Arachnoleptic Fit (n.): The frantic dance performed just after you've accidentally walked through a spider web.
- Beelzebug (n.): Satan in the form of a mosquito, that gets into your bedroom at three in the morning and cannot be cast out.
- Caterpallor (n.): The color you turn after finding half a worm in the fruit you're eating.

The Washington Post has also published the winning submissions to its yearly contest, in which readers are asked to supply alternate meanings for common words. And the winners are:
- Coffee, n. The person upon whom one coughs.
- Flabbergasted, adj. Appalled by discovering how much weight one has gained.
- Abdicate, v. To give up all hope of ever having a flat stomach.
- Esplanade, v. To attempt an explanation while drunk.
- Willy-nilly, adj. Impotent.
- Negligent, adj.. Absentmindedly answering the door when wearing only a nightgown.
- Lymph, v. To walk with a lisp.
- Gargoyle, n. Olive-flavored mouthwash.
- Flatulence, n. Emergency vehicle that picks up someone who has been run over by a steamroller.
- Balderdash, n. A rapidly receding hairline.
- Testicle, n. A humorous question on an exam.
- Rectitude, n. The formal, dignified bearing adopted by proctologists.
- Pokemon, n. A Rastafarian proctologist.
- Oyster, n. A person who sprinkles his conversation with Yiddishisms.
- Frisbeetarianism, n. The belief that, after death, the soul flies up onto the roof and gets stuck there.
- Circumvent, n. An opening in the front of boxer shorts worn by Jewish men.

Word Meanings - More

Cross country - Iran
Jigsaw - Injury caused through Irish dancing
Farming - a vase that's furthest away from you
Cabbage - taxi fare
Diversion - translation into Welsh
Pumpkin - to interrogate a member of your family
Meander - she and I
Direction - aroused Welshman
Humphrey - a road with no speed bumps
Portly - shaped like a harbour
Wench - a spanner belonging to Jonathan Ross
Wok – a fing you fwow at a wabbit when your wifle bwoke.
Mutate - an art gallery for cats
Abacus - a Swedish swear word
Paradox - quandary over which doctor to use
Tycoon - businessman who made his money selling cravats
Geriatric - fine bowling spell by a German cricketer
Rancour - Japanese term of abuse
Idiomatic - Ugandan washing machine
Circumstantial - circumcision on a really big baby
Dunderhead - what a sculptor says when he's done the top part of a statue
Psychiatric - guessing right, three times in a row
Diarrhoea - an unattractive bottom
Moustache - got to go!
Posthumous - the act of delivering Greek food by mail
Sanctity - drooping bosom
Piston - humiliated
Negligent - a man who wears lingerie
Wallaby - someone aspiring to be a Kangaroo
Miniscule - a toddler's playgroup in Liverpool
Lactose - the effect of frostbite
Fiasco - unsuccessful wall painting
Shingle - Sean Connery's definition of a bachelor
Avoidable - what a cow with a headache does

Wordplay

- Those who jump off a bridge in Paris are in Seine.
- A backward poet writes inverse.
- A man's home is his castle, in a manor of speaking
- Dijon vu - the same mustard as before.
- Practice safe eating - always use condiments.
- Shotgun wedding: A case of wife or death.
- A hangover is the wrath of grapes.
- Dancing cheek-to-cheek is really a form of floor play.
- Does the name Pavlov ring a bell?
- Reading while sunbathing makes you well red.
- When two egotists meet, it's an I for an I.
- A bicycle can't stand on its own because it is two tired.
- What's the definition of a will? (It's a dead giveaway.)
- Time flies like an arrow. Fruit flies like a banana.
- In democracy your vote counts. In feudalism your count votes.
- She was engaged to a boyfriend with a wooden leg but broke it off.
- A chicken crossing the road is poultry in motion.
- Why did he chicken cross Hollywood Boulevard? To see Gregory Peck.
- If you don't pay your exorcist, you get repossessed.
- With her marriage, she got a new name and a dress.
- When a clock is hungry, it goes back four seconds.
- The man who fell into an upholstery machine is fully recovered.
- You feel stuck with your debt if you can't budge it.
- Local Area Network in Australia: the LAN down under.
- He often broke into song because he couldn't find the key.
- Every calendar's days are numbered.
- A lot of money is tainted - It taint yours and it taint mine.
- A boiled egg in the morning is hard to beat.
- He had a photographic memory that was never developed.
- A plateau is a high form of flattery.
- A midget fortune-teller who escapes from prison is a small medium at large.
- Those who get too big for their britches will be exposed in the end.
- Once you've seen one shopping centre, you've seen a mall.

- Bakers trade bread recipes on a knead-to-know basis.
- Santa's helpers are subordinate clauses.
- … and his wife is Mary Christmas.
- Acupuncture is a jab well done

You Know When You're Living In 2018 When..

1. You accidentally enter your password on the microwave.
2. You haven't played solitaire with real cards in years.
3. You have a list of 15 phone numbers to reach your family of 3.
4. You e-mail the person who works at the desk next to you.
5. Your reason for not staying in touch with friends is that they don't have e-mail addresses.
6. When you go home after a long day at work you still answer the phone in a business manner.
7. When you make phone calls from home, you accidentally dial '1' to get an outside line.
8. You've sat at the same desk for four years and worked for three different companies.
10. You learn about your redundancy on the 11 o'clock news.
11. Your boss doesn't have the ability to do your job.
12. Contractors outnumber permanent staff and are more likely to get long-service awards.

AND..............
- You read this entire list, and kept nodding and smiling.
- As you read this list, you think about forwarding it to your 'friends.'
- You got this email from a friend that never talks to you anymore, except to send you jokes from the net.
- You are too busy to notice there was no #9.
- You actually scrolled back up to check that there wasn't a #9.
- AND NOW U R LAUGHING at yourself.

About the Author

In New Zealand I experienced life as an accountant, credit manager, company director, shepherd, scrub-cutter, tree pruner, freezing worker, plastics factory worker, saxophonist, army driver, tour bus driver, stage and television actor and singer, builder, lecturer, facilitator for men's groups, reporter, columnist, magazine editor, publisher, writer ...

In South Africa as an AIDS workshop co-facilitator ...

In the Australian bush as a barman, horse and camel trekker and stock-whip teacher ...

In England as a contract accountant, corporate trainer, estate manager, lecturer, singer/songwriter, website editor/writer and freelance writer …

Now that I'm back in Australia, house renovating, teaching and writing, I'm wondering what's next!

The constant for my wife and I is *A Course in Miracles*, a psychological life-style course in forgiveness. Through it I have found the peace I had always been searching for - the journey to where we have always been.

Philip J Bradbury in social media
Website: www.philipjbradbury.com
Wordpress blogs:
   https://flashfictionfanatic.wordpress.com/
   https://pjbradbury.wordpress.com/
Facebook:
   https://www.facebook.com/AuthorPhilipJBradbury/
Linked In - http://bit.ly/2aTzZMS
About Me: https://about.me/philipbradbury
Amazon: amzn.to/25X0CLb
Google+: http://bit.ly/2bsbpUy
Pininterest: https://au.pinterest.com/bradburywords/
Smashwords: http://bit.ly/2aNjkic
Twitter: https://twitter.com/PhilipJBradbury

The Meaning Of Larf

Philip J Bradbury

Published by   A Write Site,
Brisbane, Australia

Copyright 2017 © Philip J Bradbury

Philip J Bradbury has asserted his right under the Copyright, Designs and Patents Act 1988 to be identified as the author.

ISBN - 978-0-9954398-5-6

All rights reserved. No part of this publication may be reproduced or transmitted in any form or by any means, electronic or mechanical, including photocopying, recording or any information storage and retrieval system, without permission in writing from the publisher.

Other books by Philip J Bradbury

Non-Fiction
Life Rejuvenated
Whose Life Is It Anyway?
The Lawless Way
Change Your Life, Change Your World
The Twelve Week Miracle (with Anna Bradbury)
Understanding Men
Articles of Faith
Conversations on Your Business
Stepping Out Of Debt and Into Financial Freedom

Some-Fiction
Dactionary – the dictionary with attitude
The Meaning of Larf
53 SMILES
97 SMILES
45 Moments With Men
51 Moments With Fables

Fiction
An Olympic Challenge
The Last Stand-Down
The Royal Bank of Stories
Circles of Gold
Gerald the Great of Gorokoland

For more information on these books, see
   www.philipjbradbury.com

Disorders that more than 65 million Americans are suffering from secondary immune deficiency disorders. Cancer generates more than $100 billion a year, with one person dying of cancer every 64 seconds, about 1,350 people per day or 500,000 people per year. More than a trillion dollars has been spent and wasted in the war against cancer."

Let's, instead, try the cheapest, most effective health plan possible - laughing ... and you might even cry a little at the niceness of people. Laughing or crying, it's all good for the soul.

And, talking of cheap, all of the following words have come to me for nothing. They turn up in my computer each day and I have no idea who wrote them originally, usually. It seems to me that the universe, daily, offers us free wisdom and so few of us take the chance to learn, grow or heal from it.

'Well,' I thought, 'they come into my world, I have a giggle, and they go out again. What a shame they don't stay for longer as I still get a good larf each time I read them'. And so this book – to celebrate the (largely) anonymous geniuses we meet every day, in our homes, communities and work-places, with their quick quip, their insightful invective, their wily wisdom, to help us through another minute, hour, day or year. They know not what healing they bring to this world. Thank you from the bottom, top, sides and every other part of my heart and funny bone.

If you're out there and wish to claim some sort of royalty, please let me know ... you won't get it but you can tell me anyway!

If you want your silly wisdom to go down in posterity, also let me know for there will surely be other books – I had so much fun doing this that I just have to do it again. I'd love to include your words in the next tittivating tome.

People say 'it's no laughing matter' – the truth is that larfing certainly does matter and let's have a whole lot more of it. Oh, by the way, Larf stands for **L**earning **A**nd **R**ealising **F**reedom ... okay, I just made that up ... but you knew that, anyway!

LARF MATTERS

The meaning of life has eluded us since Pontius was a pilot, or before then, when Adam and Eve started begetting all sorts of people with unpronounceable names. In spite of all our amazing knowledge and ability to communicate, no one has come up with a definitive meaning for life – if they had there would only be one religion and one guru. As it is, the number of religions is increasing and there's a new philosophy, a new diet, a new business system and a new way of trying to be what you're not, coming out every day.

However, like riding a bike or making love, life doesn't have to be understood to be enjoyed ... in fact, those who think they have the answers (priests, philosophers, gurus) seem to have very serious faces and not a lot of fun. If that's their meaning of life, they're welcome to it. So, let's get off the need to understand anything and just have some fun, spreading some silliness through this ever-so-earnest world of ours.

What we do all know for a certainty is that the meaning of larf (or *laugh* for those who speak properly English) is larf itself. It's just good to do and we all feel better for a good larf. And larfs are contagious – you can't help larfing when someone else does and it's so easy to get others to do it – just fake a larf and they're off – the simplest and cheapest way of healing an earnest and depressed world. And, to my strange mind, health and happiness are attracted to the simplest and cheapest of remedies, while the more complex and expensive remedies seem to spawn a whole host of other problems, as Dr Bruce Halstead, Director of the World Life Research Institute, Colton, California, stated in his article *The Health Plan for the United States*:

"The bottom line is to keep America sick, as sick people make astronomical amounts of money for the medical profession. Medical care is a monopolistic industry that generates in excess of $600 billion per year, or almost 12% of the Gross National Product. It has been estimated by the coalition of Immune System

www.ingramcontent.com/pod-product-compliance
Lightning Source LLC
Chambersburg PA
CBHW070617300426
44113CB00010B/1561